Sho My Own Business?

Accurately Predict
Your Success or Failure

Sample Business Plan
Break Even Analysis
Accounting Terms Explained
Government Regulations
Much More...

First Edition

January 19, 2013

© Copyrighted

Larry Flinchpaugh

About the Author

The author, Larry Flinchpaugh, was born April 16, 1939 in St. Joseph, Missouri. His parents Johnny and Margery Flinchpaugh were owners of the "Flinchpaugh Pet Shop, Reptile Gardens and Zoo. His early years were spent working in his parents business but when he got married in 1960 and had the responsibility of raising a family, he found it more lucrative to work as an accountant for Phillips Petroleum Company. While working for Phillips in Bartlesville, Oklahoma, Larry started a part time business called "The Patio Shop" which Larry's wife Phyllis managed during the week and Larry helped in his spare time at night and on weekends and holidays.   The Patio Shop specialized in selling craft supplies and in manufacturing concrete garden statuary.

In 1976 the author was offered a job with TOSCO, The Oil and Shale Corporation as a manager of "Finished Products Inventory Control" in Bakersfield, California.

In 1983, while working for TOSCO in California, he started another business called "TV Facts", a free weekly magazine full of advertisements and coupons from local businesses. After a moderate degree of success with TV Facts, he sold his interest in the business and started another business called "Consign It Stores, Inc." Consign It Stores specialized in selling and appraising antiques and quality used furniture and provided for a liquidation service of personal property from individuals, various types of businesses and the Kern County Coroner's Office.

In 1985 he semi-retired leaving Tosco to work full time in his own business. By the time he had fully retired in 2005 and moved back to St. Joe, his business had grown to two stores with 8 employees.

The book you are about to read should help you decide if you should start your own business or work for someone else. It is hoped that reading about the experiences of the author, both good and bad, will help you make the correct decision. This could be one of the most important decisions in your life. If you do decide to become an "entrepreneur", you want to be sure it is for the right reasons and that you do all that is possible to guarantee your success.

Keep in mind as you read this book, the author probably made more money on his real estate investments than the actual businesses he started. But keep in mind he also made a good living for his family pursuing his business interests. Furthermore he had a built in margin of safety by having a good full time job with his wife operating the business until it started making money.

Although not absolutely necessary, the fact that the author had an accounting background gave him an advantage in that he did not have to hire anyone for this service.

Larry Flinchpaugh

Table of Contents

Table of Contents
(continued)

Notes:

Chapter One
Are you thinking about starting a Business?

There are many advantages of owning your own business like being your own boss, making a good living and providing for your family, doing something you really enjoy and working on your own time schedule.

However, before making such an important decision on whether you should make the leap from an employee to Entrepreneur, ask yourself, "Why do I want to do this?" Hopefully you want to start a business for the right reasons and have prepared a written *Business Plan* and a *Break Even Analysis* to calculate the feasibility of your success.

A few years ago a friend of mine told me that he was opening a Toy Store in Bakersfield, California. He was so excited that I didn't want to say anything negative that might discourage him. But I did ask him a few questions. I said, "Why do you want to open up a toy store?" His answer was "I have always liked toys and thought it would be a lot of fun selling something that I really enjoy. "Not a good reason, I thought." Then I asked him if he were going to borrow any money to get started? "Not really", "I have taken early retirement from the oil company and have enough cash to at least start a business and sustain me until it becomes profitable."

Then I asked him, "Did you create a business plan and determine your daily sales volume necessary to cover all your expenses needed to break even." He again replied, "That's not necessary because I have the money to start my business from my retirement and a Toy Shop should be pretty simple to manage." I wanted to ask him if he thought he could compete with "Toys-R-Us but decided not to. I was convinced that my friend should not be starting this business but he didn't ask for my counseling, so I remained silent. I hoped I was wrong.

I followed his progress and just as I had expected, he went out of business in only a year and a half. He lost a substantial amount of his retirement and learned a very expensive lesson.

You don't want to make the same mistakes that my friend made. Make sure you are starting a business for the right reason. First you need to ask yourself why you want to start a business. Is it simply that you want to make lots of money so you can live an extravagant life style or maybe you just want to be your own boss? Both of these reasons are legitimate and the possibility of making a lot of money is a good motivating factor. Just be sure that you don't open up a toy store because you like toys and think it would be fun to sell something you really enjoy.

In order to become successful in any business, you must have a real passion for what you are about to undertake and enjoy working with people and solving problems.

To assist you in making the correct decision, ask yourself the following questions:

- Is there a need for my business?

- Have I made a formal Business Plan?

- Have I made a list of my long range goals? Plus the short range goals to make the long range goals a reality?

- Do I have adequate experience and skills in this business to succeed?

- Can I handle my own accounting? Do I have any accounting skills, particularly with double entry accounting and Microsoft Word and Excel?

- Am I willing to work more than 40 hours per week to make my business successful?

- Am I willing to spend less time with my family to succeed?

- Can I survive without a steady income until the business becomes profitable?

- Can I find employees, and afford to pay them, with skills that I don't have?

- Do I have confidence in my ability to succeed?

- Am I able to make correct decisions quickly by analyzing the *cost* of those decisions?

- Do I have the ability to get along with different personalities; both customers and employees?

- Am I a creative person? Do I have the ability to take a lemon, and turn it into lemonade?

- Do I have a mentor that I can rely on in time of need?

The more of these questions that you can honestly answer "Yes" too, the more likely you will succeed.

You can pretty well predict if your dream of owning a business is attainable by completing a **business plan** (see appendix) and a **break even analysis**. The next chapter will explain how to accurately predict your success or failure by calculating what your daily income will need to be to cover your costs plus something left over to cover your living expenses.

If the break even analysis says that there is no way this plan can succeed because either revenue is not enough or expenses are excessive, then stop and proceed in another direction. If you are unable to fix the problems, then move on to another endeavor and try again. It is better to find out now before losing thousands of dollars of your hard earned money like my friend did with his toy store.

According to SBA statistics;

- * Seven out of 10 new employer firms survive at least 2 years
- ** Half at least 5 years
- *** A third at least 10 years
- **** A quarter stay in business 15 years or more

* In other words 30% of new businesses failed after the first two years.

** 50% of new businesses have failed within 5 years.

*** 66 2/3 fail after 10 years.

**** 75% of new businesses did not make it 15 years or more.

Census data reports that 69 percent of new employer establishments born to new firms in 2000 survived at least 2 years, and 51 percent survived 5 or more years. Survival rates were similar across states and major industries."

.

Chapter Two
First Create a Business Plan and a Break Even Analysis

The Break even analysis will help you decide if your business has any realistic chance of success. It will reveal the monthly sales amount required to cover your business expenses while the business becomes profitable. It may even tell you that your business is simply not going to work if your projected daily sales are not enough to cover your expenses. If that is the case, it is better to find out now before you invest your hard earned savings or take out a loan that will be impossible to pay.

A Break Even Analysis is really not that hard to construct. First make a list of all supposed monthly expenses:
- Monthly Rent or mortgage payment
- Light Bill
- Gas Bill
- Telephone Bill
- Advertising Expenses
- Insurance Expense
- Employee expense
- Interest Expense
- Accounting expense
- Postage Expense
- Office Supplies
- other

Second, calculate the amount of sales needed to cover these expenses based on your average profit margin for your type of business. Assume your total monthly expenses totaled $8,000. If your gross profit margin was 50% in your particular business, then you would need to sell $16,000 per month. If you opened for business approximately 26 days a month, you would need to sell $616.00 per day to break even before any profit is made.(26 days times $616.00 per day = $16,016.00)

Of course if you don't have a wife or husband with a source of income to live on while the business becomes profitable, you will need to add your living expenses to the $8,000 example shown above and recalculate the daily sales needed to cover the added living expense.

Complete your "Break Even Analysis" and Business plan before you ask a bank to make you a loan. You are much more likely to get the loan if you have a well thought out plan for your business. However, just because the bank gives you a loan to start your business doesn't mean that you have a successful plan. They are not risking anything because more than likely they will want your house or car as collateral and will be paid even if you fail.

I asked a banker once if they had any responsibility to advise you if they felt that your business was likely to fail. They said, "No." What they were actually saying was that the bank was not in the business of giving you business advice. Their main concern was, could you repay the loan and if not was there enough collateral pledged to guarantee the loan payoff if they had to foreclose on your personal property. It makes one wonder if the bank has your best interest at heart.

Whatever the source of your investment money, you must be careful to make the same decisions whether it is your money, borrowed money, or a gift. Easy money is easy to spend and most people don't make the same decisions when the investment is borrowed money rather than their own... For example, if you have ready cash of $50,000 to get started you may make an unwise decision to buy a new truck for $30,000 instead of a cheaper used truck for $10,000... It may have been wiser to buy a used truck and have money left over for other expenses even though you had the cash for a new truck.

In the appendix of this book is a sample Business Plan form for you to follow. When applying for a loan, show the lending institution both the *Break Even Analysis* and the *Business Plan*. A well thought out plan will impress them and will most assuredly help you in getting a loan. Of course if your *Break Even Analysis* shows that you are unlikely to succeed, you would then drop your project and not be embarrassed by a loan refusal. There is no need to waste either your or the banks time.

Chapter Three
Choose Your Business Structure

There are five basic forms of business structures to choose from:

- Sole Proprietorship-Most common
- Partnership
- Corporation
- Sub-Chapter S Corporation and LLC
- Cooperative

The most common business structure is a *Sole Proprietorship* where you alone own the company and are responsible for its assets and liabilities.

Advantages of a Sole Proprietorship (Ref. sba.gov website)

- **Easy and inexpensive to form**: A sole proprietorship is the simplest and least expensive business structure to establish. Costs are minimal, with legal costs limited to obtaining the necessary license or permits.
- **Complete control**. Because you are the sole owner of the business, you have complete control over all decisions. You aren't required to consult with anyone else when you need to make decisions or want to make changes.
- **Easy tax preparation**. Your business is not taxed separately, so it's easy to fulfill the tax reporting requirements for a sole proprietorship. The tax rates are also the lowest of the business structures.

Disadvantages of a Sole Proprietorship (Ref. sba.gov website)

- **Unlimited personal liability**. Because there is no legal separation between you and your business, you can be held personally liable for the debts and obligations of the business. This risk extends to any liabilities incurred as a result of employee actions.

- **Hard to raise money**

  Sole proprietors often face challenges when trying to raise money. Because you can't sell stock in the business, investors won't often invest. Banks are also hesitant to lend to a sole proprietorship because of a perceived lack of credibility when it comes to repayment if the business fails.

- **Heavy burden.**

  The flipside of complete control is the burden and pressure it can impose. You alone are ultimately responsible for the successes and failures of your business.

Partnerships

There are several different types of *partnerships* depending on the responsibilities of each partner and the amount of money they have invested and the amount of time, if any, they are expected to work in the business. It is wise to have an attorney prepare legal agreements for each partner. Remember, each partner is responsible for the other partner's actions.

One partner may be left holding the bag when another partner racks up thousands of dollars of personal expenses charged to the business, and then disappears with the office secretary and moves to South America. The remaining partners are then responsible for his mis-deeds. This is the reason this why I would advise you to avoid this type of business arrangement. It is enticing because the partners will supply part of the startup costs and risk, but remember, they also share in the profits. Numerous problems arise in a partnership, many resulting in the partners suing each other in court.

Corporation

A *corporation* is more complex and usually applies to large companies with many employees. "A corporation (sometimes referred to as a C corporation) is an independent legal entity owned by shareholders. This means that the corporation itself, not the shareholders that own it, is held legally liable for the actions and debts the business incurs. Corporations are more complex than other business structures because they tend to have costly administrative fees and complex tax and legal requirements. Because of these issues, corporations are generally suggested for established, larger companies with multiple employees.

For businesses in that position, corporations offer the ability to sell ownership shares in the business through stock offerings...."

(Ref. sba.gov website)

Advantages of a Corporation (Ref. sba.gov website)

- **Limited Liability.** When it comes to taking responsibility for business debts and actions of a corporation, shareholders' personal assets are protected. Shareholders can generally only be held accountable for their investment in stock of the company.
- **Ability to Generate Capital.** Corporations have an advantage when it comes to raising capital for their business - the ability to raise funds through the sale of stock.
- **Corporate Tax Treatment.** Corporations file taxes separately from their owners. Owners of a corporation only pay taxes on corporate profits paid to them in the form of salaries, bonuses, and dividends, while any additional profits are awarded a corporate tax rate, which is usually lower than a personal income tax rate.
- **Attractive to Potential Employees.** Corporations are generally able to attract and hire high-quality and motivated employees because they offer competitive

benefits and the potential for partial ownership through stock options.

Disadvantages of a Corporation

- **Time and Money.** Corporations are costly and time-consuming ventures to start and operate. Incorporating requires start-up, operating and tax costs that most other structures do not require.
- **Double Taxing.** In some cases, corporations are taxed twice - first, when the company makes a profit, and again when dividends are paid to shareholders.
- **Additional Paperwork.** Because corporations are highly regulated by federal, state, and in some cases local agencies, there are increased paperwork and recordkeeping burdens associated with this entity.

Sub-Chapter S Corporation (Ref. sba.gov website)
"An S corporation (sometimes referred to as an S Corp) is a special type of corporation created through an IRS tax election. An eligible domestic corporation can avoid double taxation (once to the corporation and again to the shareholders) by electing to be treated as an S corporation.

An S corp is a corporation with the Subchapter S designation from the IRS. To be considered an S corp, you must first charter a business as a corporation in the state where it is headquartered. According to the IRS, S corporations are "considered by law to be a unique entity, separate and apart from those who own it." This limits the financial liability for which you (the owner or "shareholder" is responsible. Nevertheless, liability protection is limited - S corps do not necessarily shield you from all litigation such as an employee's tort actions as a result of a workplace incident.

What makes the S Corp different from a traditional corporation (C Corp) is that profits and losses can pass through to your personal tax return. Consequently, the business is not taxed itself. Only the shareholders are taxed. There is an important caveat, however: any shareholder who works for the company must pay him or herself "reasonable compensation." Basically, the shareholder must be paid fair market value, or the IRS might reclassify any additional corporate earnings as "wages." (Ref. sba.gov website)

There are sources of help on the internet to help you file the papers yourself for a subchapter S corporation or you may want to have your CPA do the set up and filing for you. It is not that complicated but it does involve quite a bit of preparation time. First you must determine if you qualify, then elect officers; President, Secretary, and Treasurer. You might wish to be the president and your wife secretary and son or daughter the treasurer. You will need to construct a corporate charter and agree to have periotic meetings with complete notes of the meetings.

Limited liability Corporation (LLC) (Ref. sba.gov website)
"There is always the possibility of requesting S Corp status for your LLC. Your attorney can advise you on the pros and cons. You'll have to make a special election with the IRS to have the LLC taxed as an S Corp using Form 2553. And you must file it before the first two months and fifteen days of the beginning of the tax year in which the election is to take effect.

The LLC remains a limited liability company from a legal standpoint, but for tax purposes it's treated as an S corp. Be sure to contact your state's income tax agency where you will file the election form to learn about tax requirements."

Cooperative (Ref. sba.gov website)

A cooperative is a business or organization owned by and operated for the benefit of those using its services. Profits and earnings generated by the cooperative are distributed among the members, also known as user-owners.

Typically, an elected board of directors and officers run the cooperative while regular members have voting power to control the direction of the cooperative. Members can become part of the cooperative by purchasing shares, though the amount of shares they hold does not affect the weight of their vote.

Cooperatives are common in the healthcare, retail, agriculture, art and restaurant industries. The Small Business Administration has a complete description on setting up a cooperative at www.sba.gov.

Whichever type of business entity you choose, it is best to first consult an attorney or CPA. (Certified Public Accountant) for guidance.

Chapter Four
Choose a Name and have it Registered

Names that I hate are those that were chosen just so they could be mentioned first in the   phone book; like ABC Cab Company or Acme radio. I suppose this was a good idea before the internet and websites were invented.   Today, many people merely "Google" the service wanted and the web browser will find your website or telephone number.

If you're starting a new business, coming up with the *perfect* name is the single most important step to getting started off on the right foot, except of course, after you have completed your **Business Plan** and **Break Even Analysis**.   Try to select a name that is catchy, tells a lot about your business, and is small enough to put on a sign.   I always laugh when I see the "International House of Pancakes" changed to "IHOP"

Going to an internet domain registering site is not the best way to pick a business name.   There are companies on the internet that claim that for a small fee will assist you in getting that perfect name. They will scour *the internet* for you to find the best business name and matching domain name for your particular business. Some will even design a logo. I prefer to use a local graphic artist and someone that understands how to create a domain name that will maximize your exposure.   Maybe you can create a name yourself but don't be afraid to get professional help if needed. It's a good idea to check the *U.S. Copyright* website to see if someone has copyrighted the name you wish to use.

The easiest name to pick is your own name like J. C. Whitney did when he started his company, "J.C. Whitney and Company," one of the largest suppliers of mail order auto parts. You can use your own last name plus adding a made up name like George Eastman did when he started his camera company, Eastman Kodak in 1888. George Eastman has been quoted as saying that the letter *k* was his favorite letter; "It seems a strong, incisive sort of letter." He and his mother devised the name **Kodak** with an Anagrams set. George Eastman said that there were three principal concepts he used in creating the name:

- It should be short,
- Easy to pronounce
- Not resemble any other name or be associated with anything else

Whatever name you choose be sure to "Google" it to be sure no one else is using that name.

Virtually all successful businesses today have a web site and you definitely don't want to be the exception. Register your company name with one of the on-line Domain Name Registering Companies. It normally will cost less than fifty dollars a year. Be on guard for a rival and more expensive company, to notify you early that your domain name registration is about to expire.

Years ago I heard of an individual going to South America and registering the name Coca Cola and Coke. He then waited until the Coca Cola Company started building plants in those countries so he could sell them the right to use that name there that he owned. Whether that was true or not, I decided to try something like that here in this country when I first heard of a new domain extension **[.TV]**. Up until that time there were only **[.com]**, **[.net]** and a couple more. I reasoned that eventually the local TV stations would want their own call letters on the **[.TV]** domain, so I registered them hoping that sometime in the future they would buy them from me for a handsome profit. This didn't happen in three years, so I dropped paying for the registration.

Remember Your Business Name Tells Your Customers:

- ## The size of your company and if you are well established

- ## Your company's values

- ## The quality of your products or service

It is imperative that you give the customer the impression that you are well established and can be trusted. To help achieve this, I did a short promotion on TV, even though it was extremely expensive. A short time later, a customer trusted my new business with over $30,000 of his antiques to sell on consignment. After I had sold all his things, I asked him how he decided to trust me and feel comfortable that I would not abscond with his valuable antiques. He replied, "I saw your ads on TV and I saw the article in the paper when you first opened and you looked very professional. I wasn't concerned." No matter what business you create, it is extremely important to develop trust and confidence in your customers mind so that they will feel comfortable in doing business with you.

I incorporated my business as a sub-chapter S corporation. That alone added some prestige. People were constantly asking if the store was part of a chain of consignment stores. It wasn't but that was a nice impression for them to have.

It helped make the stores look professional and trustworthy.

Which name gives you the best impression of the authors' consignment stores?

Consign It Stores

Or

Consign It Stores Inc.

Chapter Five
Obtain a Business License and Permits

Any name other than your own personal name will need to be registered with the authorities. The appropriate government agencies will require you to file a declaration called a DBA (Doing Business As). This allows the authorities the ability to verify the true owners of a business. In other words, the business cannot be owned by Mr. Anonymous. It must be registered. Contact the IRS to get a Federal Id number or in some cases you can use your personal Social Security number. However, it is recommended that you obtain a Federal ID number. The Federal ID number will need to be used on all quarterly Federal Tax Reports, estimated tax payments and yearly Income tax filings. Your particular state may assign you a separate state ID number.

If applicable, your state will require you to obtain a *Resale Identification number* to use when reporting to them sales tax collected by your business. Also this number is used to show your wholesale supplier that you are exempt from paying him sales tax because your purchases are for resale.

When the author first started his business in California, the state wanted a thousand dollar deposit to insure the state that they would get paid in the event his business went broke. He didn't feel that this was fair for him to be penalized for something that might happen, so he refused. The state authorities advised him that he would not be permitted to open up his business without this resale number. Larry responded with, "There must be another solution. I cannot afford to loan the state a thousand dollars." Finally they informed him that it could be waived if he were bonded. It cost him $60 to be bonded which was much easier than coming up with another $1,000.

Your local city or county government may require special licenses or permits pertaining to safety and health issues.

Some of these will seem unfair and ridiculous but you have no choice other than to put up with them.

In Bakersfield, California, I was given a warning citation for not getting a permit to string up those bright red, yellow and white triangle plastic pennants around my parking lot to attract attention.

The reasoning by the city was that businesses put them up and then fail to take them down and they then weather and become an eye sore.

I thought this was ridiculous so called the city code enforcement to complain. When the supervisor answered the phone, I identified myself as the business getting the warning citation and was requesting what time the cities *pennant police* stopped working on Friday and what time did they start working on Monday. He informed that the officer clocked out at 5 PM on Friday and clocked in at 8 AM Monday. I then replied, "What is the likelihood of me getting caught without a pennant permit if I put up my pennants at 5:30 Friday and then take them down at 7:30 Monday morning. The supervisor started laughing and said I most likely wouldn't get caught. I said, thank you and hung up.

Again in Bakersfield California, I was warned that I could not *give* my customers free popcorn that I had popped with a commercial popper unless I had a city health permit. Being a little disgusted, I said, "Oh, I understand. I did read in the paper a few days ago that there have been quite a few cases of popcorn poisoning in the city lately. The inspector was not amused by my sarcastic remark. I also wanted to know why the local churches did not need a permit to *sell* their popcorn. Again he was not amused and fortunately left with me getting only a warning. I had the feeling that he thought I had made some good points. All future free popcorn was popped in the store room and covertly given to only known customers whom the store employees knew were not undercover popcorn enforcement cops.

I am making light of these illustrations to give a perspective business owner some examples of what they will encounter. You can see that there is some validity to the city's code enforcement policies, but they are still sometimes a nuisance to the business owner. These are examples of government regulations that all business people must put up with.

Also be aware that there is a federal law requiring handicap parking spaces and handicap restrooms in all business establishments. You would think that old historic buildings would be exempt because of excessive costs to retro fit the old building to current standards. They are not. A friend of mine could not open his business in an old Victorian house because it was going to cost him several thousand dollars to make the bathroom accessible for a wheel chair.

A small police equipment supply business near my store was required to have two handicap parking spaces when there was only a total of five parking spaces available on their property. The business owners tried to explain to code enforcement that none of their customers were handicapped policemen buying uniforms, guns, batons and other police equipment. No one would listen and refused to make an exception for these unusual circumstances.

These examples of code enforcements are pointed out to warn a prospective business owner to not sign any contracts until they know if they can afford to conform to all the federal, state, city and country requirements.

In review, the following is a list of license and permits that you will most likely encounter in order to open up your new business:

- Doing Business As Registration (DBA).
- Federal ID Number from the IRS (Internal Revenue Service).
- State ID Number from your state
- State Resale permit number from your state
- Miscellaneous governmental licenses and permits regarding safety and health issues.

Registering your DBA is done either with your County Clerk's office or with your state government, depending on where your business is located. There are a few states that do not require the registering of fictitious business names. (Reference sba.gov web site)

Federal Licenses & Permits

The following information may be found in more detail on the www.sba.gov website:

If your business is involved in activities supervised and regulated by a federal agency – such as selling alcohol, firearms, commercial fishing, etc. – then you may need to obtain a federal license or permit. Here is a brief list of business activities that require these forms and information on how to apply.

Agriculture

If you import or transport animals, animal products, biologics, biotechnology or plants across state lines, you'll need to apply for a permit from the U.S. Department of Agriculture (USDA).

Alcoholic Beverages

If you manufacture, wholesale, import, or sell alcoholic beverages at a retail location, you will need to register your business and obtain certain federal permits (for tax purposes) with the U.S. Treasury's Alcohol and Tobacco Tax and Trade Bureau (TTB). The website has a number of online tools that make this process straightforward. If you are just starting a business in this trade, start by reading the TTB's New Visitors Guide which offers helpful information for small business owners.

Remember, you will also need to contact your local Alcohol Beverage Control Board for local alcohol business permit and licensing information.

Aviation

Does your business involve the operation of aircraft; the transportation of goods or people via air; or aircraft maintenance? If so, you'll need to apply for one or more of the following licenses and certificates from the Federal Aviation Administration:

- FAA Licenses and Certificates - Get licensing information for airmen, aircraft, airports, airlines and medical aviation services.
- Pilot Licenses and Training Requirements
- Aircraft Mechanic Licenses

Firearms, Ammunition and Explosives

Businesses who manufacture, deal and import firearms, ammunitions and explosives must comply with the Gun Control Act's licensing requirements. The Act is administered by the Bureau of Alcohol, Tobacco, Firearms and Explosives (ATF). Refer to the following resources from the ATF to make sure your business is properly licensed:

- Firearms Industry Guide – Includes information on obtaining and renewing a federal firearms license, importing firearms and ammunitions, and more.
- Explosives Industry Guide – Find out how to get a federal explosives license.
- How to Become a Federal Firearms Licensee (FFL)
- How to Become a Federal Explosives Licensee (FEL)

Fish and Wildlife

If your business is engaged in any wildlife related activity, including the import/export of wildlife and derivative products, must obtain an appropriate permit from the U.S. Fish and Wildlife Service.

Commercial Fisheries

Commercial fishing businesses are required to obtain a license for fishing activities from the NOAA Fisheries Service. This guide includes quick links to permit applications and information.

Maritime Transportation

If you provide ocean transportation or facilitate the shipment of cargo by sea, you'll need to apply here for a license from the Federal Maritime Commission.

Mining and Drilling

Businesses involved in the drilling for natural gas, oil or other mineral resources on federal lands may be required to obtain a drilling permit from the Bureau of Ocean Energy Management, Regulation and Enforcement (formerly the Minerals Management Service).

Nuclear Energy

Producers of commercial nuclear energy and fuel cycle facilities as well as businesses involved in the distribution and disposal of nuclear materials must apply for a license from the U.S. Nuclear Regulatory Commission

Radio and Television Broadcasting

If your business broadcasts information by radio, television, wire, satellite and cable, you may be required to obtain a license from The Federal Communications Commission (FCC).

Transportation and Logistics

If you operate an oversize or overweight vehicle, you'll need to abide by the U.S. Department of Transportation offers guidelines on maximum weight. Permits for oversize / overweight vehicles are issued by your state government. Get contact information here.

State Licenses & Permits (Reference sba.gov web site)

Starting a business? Confused about whether you need a business license or permit?

Virtually every business needs some form of license or permit to operate legally. However, licensing and permit requirements vary depending on the type of business you are operating, where it's located, and what government rules apply.

To help you identify the specific licenses or permits your business may need, use SBA.gov's Permit Me tool. Simply enter your zip code and business type to view a list of the licenses or permits you'll need, together with information and links to the application process.

.

Chapter Six
Financing Your Business

There are several ways to finance your business:

- Banks
- Savings and Loans
- Credit Unions
- Credit Cards
- Personal Loans

Banks

Which is the best for you? The bank is the most obvious and the fact that you have prepared a *Business Plan* and a *Break Even Analysis* will greatly improve your chances to obtain a loan from them. But, I want to caution you on two aspects of getting a bank loan. As I said earlier in the book, the bank is not in the business of giving you advice. They may privately think that you have little chance of success. All they are interested in is, "Can you repay the loan?" And if not, that is no problem for them because they, more than likely, had you put up your house, car and children as collateral.

If you do get a bank loan, it is a good idea to have an attorney read the fine print. I didn't do this when I got a somewhat large loan of over $200,000 from Wells Fargo. I didn't feel that I needed an attorney because the loan officer was a neighbor and a friend and surely, I thought "Wells Fargo would not have me sign anything that was not in my best interest." I was wrong. Very wrong. My mistake cost me $10,000. In the fine print of Wells Fargo loan documents, I had agreed to an early loan payoff penalty. I didn't remember reading that but even if I did, there was little chance of me paying off this large loan early. Again I was wrong. I sold the property a few years later and was confronted with a payoff penalty of $10,000. What was really disgusting, after talking to other loan officers of other institution, I discovered this part of the loan can usually be either eliminated or at least applied to only those loans paid off 1-2 years after the loan was made. I learned to not trust even a bank like Wells Fargo. I have often wondered how much of a commission my so called friend received for tricking me into signing such a loan document with heavy pre-payment penalties.

Many years ago, I needed $30,000 to build a metal building on a vacant lot I had purchased. At first the loan office at the bank refused to make the loan. I said to him, "You didn't approve the loan because you don't know anything about me or what my plans are for the future. Come out to my business tomorrow and let me give you a tour of what I am doing." He agreed and after taking the tour and seeing my plans, he authorized the loan. At this time I had not even heard of a written B*usiness Plan* or a *Break Even Analysis* but in effect my tour accomplished the same thing. Don't make this same mistake. If you are starting a business prepare a *Business Plan* and a *Break Even Analysis*.

Savings and Loans and Credit Unions

I have never borrowed from a Savings and Loan but have had good luck with my Credit Union. Credit Unions sometimes have lower interest rates and are a little more flexible than a bank. I needed to borrow $6,000 a few years ago to purchase a vacant lot to start a small business while working for Phillips 66. I only needed $6,000 but fortunately the lot appraised for $10,000. The Credit Union agreed to loan me 75% of the appraised value or $7500. I had $1500 extra to install a chain link fence and build a small portable office building on skids. At the time, I thought this was quite a profitable process and hoped that I could use this idea again in the future. This is what is referred to as using **OPM** (Other People's money).

Credit Cards

I don't recommend Credit Cards as a way to finance business expenses because of the high interest rates usually associated with them. But sometimes you can get a line of credit on one with reasonable interest rates. This gives you an immediate source for borrowing in emergencies without the need of going through a lengthy loan application process. The danger is that it is so easy to get money this way; you may end up of having a huge balance on your business credit card. Be extremely cautious and use it only when it is absolutely necessary.

Personal Loans

I would advise you not to borrow money from friends and relatives. If a commercial loan company or bank will not loan you money, there most certainly is a good reason. If you fail you will lose your friends and never be trusted again by your relatives. It is best to avoid getting into this uncomfortable and embarrassing position.

However it is sometimes extremely advantageous to borrow from another business person who owns property that you need for your business. Almost immediately after starting my business in 1981 it had expanded so that my 3,000 square foot store front in a shopping mall was no longer sufficient.

Soon, I found a 13,000 square foot building on a major intersection in Bakersfield, California that was listed for $375,000. There was no way I could borrow that kind of money from the bank. I decided to contact the owner directly since the property was no longer listed by a real estate broker and see if he would finance the property himself. He lived in Los Angeles but agreed to meet me in Bakersfield at my business location. I showed him the lay out of my current business and explained why I needed his larger building.

He had to get back to Los Angeles and said he would call me the next day. He invited my wife and me to meet him and his interpreter at a Marie Callendars Restaurant in Los Angeles two days later. He didn't speak English very well because he had just recently moved to the U.S. from Taiwan.

I explained to him that I would offer him $350,000 instead of the $375,000 if he would carry the loan with no money down. I explained that I had $20,000 cash but that would be needed to get the building ready for me to occupy it; heating and air conditioning, carpet, painting, new doors, etc. I also pointed out, that if I defaulted he would be getting $20,000 of building improvements. I wasn't sure that line of reasoning would work but it was worth a try. It really depends on had badly someone wants to sell their property.

He thought for a moment and said he had to stay at $375,000 but would finance the property for 20 years at 12% interests. (12% was the going rate at this time) He also said that he would amortize* the loan for 20 years but wanted a balloon payment to pay off the loan in ten years. I thought that was reasonable because in 10 years I should have enough equity in the property to get a conventional loan from a bank. I said, "One more thing. I would like to not have the first loan payment due for 60 days after the loan closes and no interest to accrue for this two month period. He stood up and shook hands with me to finalize the deal. All that was left was to have a formal contract written up by the escrow company.

As my wife and I were driving back to Bakersfield late that night, I commented, "Do you realize what we have just done? We purchased a $375,000 piece of real estate with no money down and don't have to make a payment for the first two months. With a mortgage payment of $3800 per month that one concession made us $7600.00. And to top it off the Drug Store that leases the one third of the building pays us $2100.00 per month. The Drug Store is paying for a large part of our mortgage payment."

We would never have been able to get a loan like this through a bank. All those books I bought years ago about *How to Buy Real Estate With No Money Down* and H*ow to Buy Real Estate For Pennies on the Dollar* certainly paid off.

This example is to show you that real estate can be bought with no money down if you can bypass the bank.

This happened in 1982 when personal computers were starting to become not only affordable but also more user friendly. I was able to find a free amortization program and printed out a 20 year payment schedule showing amounts paid and the current balance. Previously I would have had to request my banker to create a table. Now, I had the ability to create my own enabling me to experiment with various interest rates and loan payment amounts in order to determine the most affordable way to go.

Chapter Seven
Choices of Location and Equipment

Choices of Location

Don't worry about paying a real estate agent a commission to find you a location for your business. They are professionals and will work hard to help you get the best possible deal. However, you may get a better deal working with the seller directly.

Ok, considering that your Break Even Analysis showed that you could reasonably have a chance of breaking even with X amount of daily sales to cover your monthly expenses. The bank where you applied for a loan was impressed with your business plan and loaned you the amount needed to get started. You had an adequate amount saved and with what your wife or husband earns you should be able to meet all personal expenses for at least two years.

If you are planning to start a business that you don't know a lot about, just for instance a Pizza Parlor, it would be a good idea to get a part time job with a Pizza Shop so you can learn the business.

I wouldn't even think of opening up a small Pizza parlor, Grocery store Convenience store, etc. unless my long term goal was to someday own a nationwide chain of stores. If you choose a business like a "Dollar Store," make it your goal to own several stores after you are successful in the first one. If you don't have big dreams like this, you may as well work for someone else. It is much more secure and gives you more quality time to spend with your family. Remember, owning a business isn't for everyone.

My first business that I started was in Bartlesville, Oklahoma while I worked for Phillips Petroleum Company. I saw an ad in Popular Science magazine that said "turn Concrete into Gold." That really intrigued me. It was an ad for the Concrete Machinery Mold Company located in Hickory, North Carolina. They sold metal molds to make concrete bird baths, fountains, and several varieties of animals including life size deers. The aluminum molds were quite expensive but it only took about one dollars'

27

worth of sand and cement to make a $20 bird bath. Later I learned to make rubber molds myself from cheap non copyrighted frogs, turtles, elves, etc. figurines purchase from the dime store. It didn't cost much money in material, but it cost a great deal of time making the mold; usually 2-3 weeks.

The problem was, I didn't have a commercial property to manufacture and sell. I began making concrete statuary in my back yard and advertising it for sale in the classified garage sale section of the local paper. My two young sons even went door to door selling a small cement frog that we made for a dollar each. This was in 1968 in our small town of just 30,000 people where, we felt perfectly safe permitting our 5 and 6 year old sons' to act as junior salesmen. It was a great lesson for them. They even were allowed to keep the amount collected from the sales. It worked fairly well until one of my neighbors complained that I was operating a business in my home which resulted in the city shutting down our home business.

I had saved up only $2,000 and that was not nearly enough to buy a piece of property or for that matter enough to pay the first and last months' rent on a commercial location. Also I knew that I would have additional expenses in other startup costs. Additional inventory to add to my own manufactured items would be needed because there was only a limited amount of items I could manufacture while working full time at Phillips.

Everything looked pretty hopeless until one morning on the way to work, I spotted a vacant lot for sale on Nowata Road; one of the busy highways coming into Bartlesville, Oklahoma. It had a small drive way off the highway that ran between two service stations and behind one of them. I wrote down the real estate broker's telephone number and gave them a call that evening. The broker came to our house and informed us that the owner wanted $10,000 for the lot. That was way more than I had plus it didn't have a building on it. My wife said, "Make him an offer of $5,000" and I quickly responded that it was not likely that the owner would agree. The real estate broker informed us that it was very unlikely but he was legally bound to write it up and present it to his client. The next day the broker called and said that the offer had been accepted.

Now what was I to do? We had put down $500.00 in earnest money and I sure hated to lose that if we couldn't come up with the five thousand. We would have to see if we could borrow at least 3 or 4 thousand dollars. I went to the credit union and they sent out an appraiser to appraise the lot. I couldn't believe that it appraised for $10,000. They told me that they would loan us 75% of the appraisal value which came to $7500.00. So we used $5,000 of it for the lot and the rest was used to build a small $1,000 office on skids and a chain link fence area to lock up the statuary. The only other expense we had was for a sign in the drive way, a city license and a light pole to service the building. Not only had we purchased a piece of real estate with no money down, we even got a large enough loan to finance the startup costs of our business. As the Branson, Missouri Comedian Yakov Smirnoff would say, "What a country." I thought at the time that maybe I could use this same technique again but on a more expensive piece of property. Little did I know at the time, I would later do something similar when I moved to California.

After our business began to be successful, I thought how I could expand it using the existing facility which would mean little or no additional expense. I came up with the idea of installing wood and chain link fences. Since I knew nothing about this business, I contacted an older gentleman who had been in the fence business for years and asked him if he would tell me some of his secrets. I think he was flattered and he agreed to help me. He showed me how to make a large square out of string to make the corners square and how to install a gate. He explained that most people left a hole for the gate and then built the gate to fit the hole.

He instructed me to first set all four posts and nail all the wood on plus mount the hinges, then simply cut out the gate. Everything fits because you made it all in one piece. This was a great time saver.

The fence experience taught me to always seek help and advice from the experts and even work for them for a few months if necessary to learn the tricks of the trade that would help me to become successful.

I didn't make a lot of money when I had to sell the property in 1976 and move to California to work for TOSCO but, I learned a lot about buying real-estate and starting a business on a shoe string. Not only did I sell the property, I carried part of the loan for the new buyer. I thought I just might as well collect interest instead of the bank. There was little risk to me because if the buyer defaulted on the loan, I would just resell it. The profit I made from the sale of the real estate in 1976 made it possible for me to move from a $21,000 house in Oklahoma to a $50,000 house in California. (I sold the California house in 2005 for $270,000.) Even though I complain about our unconstitutional and evil banking system, I was able to take advantage of the inflationary aspects of it to realize a healthy profit.

Once I got to California and was working for TOSCO as an accounting manager, I started thinking again about starting another business. I saw an ad in a magazine that for $10,000 you could acquire a franchise from a company called "TV Facts.' This weekly magazine was a superior local TV guide that was distributed free at the local super markets. They recommended that you have $800.00 worth of weekly paid advertising contracted for before printing your first issue.

I just couldn't resist the temptation of getting back into business and this time it was with a partner. As I said earlier I don't recommend partnerships but this one did work out fairly well even though we didn't make a lot of money. At least I was able to learn a lot about advertising which would help me in my future business adventures. My business partner, who was also my boss at the oil company, and I finally, with a great deal of effort, presold $400.00 worth of advertisement and started with our first issue hoping to add more revenue later. I still don't know how we ever sold any ads before the book was even published. We did have a nice sample of books from other areas of the country to show our clients.

One effective sales gimmick that we used was to sign people up for an eight week advertising *agreement*; we were advised by the Franchisor to call it an *agreement* instead of a *contract*. It is psychologically easier to get someone to sign an *agreement* than it is a *contract*. It worked, plus with an eight week commitment we didn't have the chore of convincing our client every week to continue advertising. As an incentive to sign up for eight weeks of ads, we offered them what we called the 5, 2, 1 plan. As a reward for signing up for eight weeks, they would receive five ads at the size they agreed to and two ads double that size and one larger ad; all for the originally agreed on price of the smaller ad. That one selling gimmick was probably the most important tool we had that insured our success. My partner and I didn't make a great deal of money in this venture but we did enjoy a few ad trade outs with a few restaurants and other business establishments.

In the beginning, it was sometimes difficult to talk a grocery store into allowing us to set up a distribution rack at their front door or to put our magazines on their crowded checkout counter. One major super market chain refused our several attempts to get them to distribute our magazine. A few days later I talked two or three of my friends into calling the super market and telling the manager that they had found a wonderful free TV guide at one of their competitors and wondered if they were going to offer it in their store. The manager was very polite and said he would look into it. A couple of days later I would again ask the store manager if he would allow us to set up a free distribution point in his store. He said, "Go ahead; I have had people calling and asking for it." I felt a little devious but it did work.

Our "TV Facts "office location, for this type of business, wasn't critical because we didn't have walk in customers.

A completely different situation arose after purchasing the super market building in Bakersfield, California for our furniture store which did have walk in traffic. I had to cut two large holes for display windows and one large hole for a double door entry in the front of the building. Wanting to look professional I installed modern aluminum frame doors just like the ones you see on the shops at the shopping center. It made a great first impression and I know greatly added to our success because of the professional image it projected.

Buying Equipment

If you are opening up a business like a Pizza parlor and need commercial refrigeration units and ovens, try to attend one of the industry trade shows to meet several different manufacturers and see demonstrations of their equipment. If there are no shows within your time frame, visit their factories in person and get real live demonstrations.

An internet search can locate many possible suppliers but it is a good idea also to start subscribing to trade magazine a few months or even a year before you start your business.

It is likely that your equipment supplier will have information available about running a successful Pizza parlor. After all, their success depends on your success.

Chapter Eight
Employee Hiring and Training

"When I needed to hire an employee, I would sometimes call a temporary agency. If they sent someone who did a good job, I would ask them to come back the next day. If they did a poor job, I simply thanked them and waited a couple of days and requested another temp. If that person did a good job after a week or two, I would offer them a full time job. I used this system several times and it worked perfectly.

It's possible to even get free help, at least for a short time. I purchased a 13,000 square foot building in California that had formerly been a Mayfair Super market. Two thirds of the building was filled with dirt from a previous storm, abandoned contractor supplies, old office equipment and a room full of heavy steel tables used to support refrigeration equipment. I could see that it was going to cost several thousand dollars to hire a crew and trash truck to clean out the building. One of my friends was a teacher for the local high school and informed me that he had a special class of students that were being trained on how to work and get a job. He volunteered to bring a large trash truck and 10 students to clean out the building. That was great. My only cost was for buying pizza and drinks after they were finished. The state took care of all the insurance, including Workman's Comp Insurance, so there was no risk of me getting into trouble if a student got injured.

After I had my business opened for a few months, an employee from a state social service agency came into my store and asked if I was currently hiring. I said that I was looking for a delivery and maintenance person but hadn't been able to find one. She informed me that they had a person they would like to recommend and that the state would pay the first three months of his salary while he was being trained. I thought that was an offer to good to refuse. The next day, I interviewed the young man in my office. He sure didn't look like a likely candidate. He was only about 5' 2" tall and didn't appear to be able to lift a sofa over his head to take it from our show room to the delivery truck. I wasn't sure that he understood everything I was telling him about the job. He was Vietnamese and had been in this country for only a year and a half. If I did hire him, I would need to be able to communicate with him and I was certain that I couldn't learn how to speak Vietnamese. But since the state was paying his first three months' salary, I decided to take a chance on hiring him.

The first day I decided to give him a few tasks to do and then evaluate his performance. I had been repairing a heavy metal door in our work shop that had loosened all three of its hinges. I explained to Tom that we needed to remove the hinges from the wall, drill out the screw holes, insert a dowel rod, re-drill the screw holes, and then remount the door. I said, "Do you understand?" He just looked at me and nodded. I thought, "This isn't going to work."

An hour later, I went back to check on his progress and was surprised that he was almost finished. I had been waiting for him to come and get me to help him lift the heavy door up so the hinges would line up with the new holes. He figured out how to do the lifting without any help. Tom had put a small block of wood on the floor and then put a crowbar under the door and used the wood block to make a lever that could be pushed with one foot, lifting the heavy door while he inserted new screws. I was really impressed.

Ok, now let's see how he does on the next project. I was drilling additional holes in a bookcase so I could add a few more shelves. The trick was to not drill completely through the walls of the bookcase, but only half way; just deep enough to support the shelf pegs. A short time later I returned to see how he was doing. He was done so I expected to see at least one hole where he had miscalculated and drilled through the whole side of the bookcase. It looked perfect. I said, "Tom. How did you do that?" He smiled and again didn't say anything and showed me the drill bit. He had wrapped a layer of masking tape around the bit at the precise depth that would not allow the bit to drill further than one half the width of the bookcase wall. Again I was impressed! This young man was a problem solver. I had made a wise choice; one that I would not have made without the states assistance program.

Tom worked for me for several years; all the time going to college part time to get a degree in computer science. Today he is a successful computer programmer with an excellent job. It's nice knowing that I may have had something to with his success by giving him his first job in America and giving him the opportunity to prove himself. But I know that he was a survivor who would have been successful even without my help.

Another way to get good help is to hire someone that you see is already doing excellent work in another job. There is an ethical problem here because you don't want to steal another company's employee. I had been impressed with the girl that worked at the Post Office Annex in our same building. I reasoned that it would be fine if she would work for me part time and in that way I wouldn't be stealing her from the Post Office. I was in need of an office manager but wasn't sure if I could afford someone of her caliber. Surely she would demand more of a salary than I could afford. I hired her anyway and did have to pay her a few dollars more than minimum wage. However, she had so many skills that she immediately paid her own way. I hated handling the quarterly tax reports and writing payroll checks. This was a job that Wendy enjoyed and was very good at. She had never had any formal training using the Micro Soft Excel work sheet or Word processor, but after I showed her what little I knew, she was off and running. I sent Wendy to a class on designing web pages and a few months later she had designed a beautiful web page for our business.

There were times that our sales were slow and I sure didn't want to lay Wendy off. She then said, "Larry why don't you allow me to put some of our merchandise on EBay?" We had a store just full of interesting collectables, etc. With a post office in the same building, it was easy for us to mail items that had been sold. In a short time, Wendy was averaging $2-3,000 in internet sales per month. This more than paid for her salary. A good employee is not an expense but rather is an investment.

Out of desperation and time constraints, I once hired an English major for an accounting job while working for TOSCO. This was something I would not have normally done, but I knew an English major could handle the job. It consisted mainly of balancing exchange accounts of gasoline and diesel. In the oil business, oil companies exchange products as well as buying and selling. After working for me for about a year, and doing an excellent job,

Jim regrettably told me that he would be leaving our department, taking a job within our own company as the writer and publisher for the company magazine. I assured him that it was fine with me and I wished him luck in his new job. His unlikely chance, being an English major, of getting hired for an accounting job had really worked well for both of us. I filled a job opening that was desperately needed at the time and Jim got his foot in the door so he could take advantage of a later opportunity. It was a win win situation for both of us. A few years ago I got a call from Jim and he said, "Larry, do you know what today is?" I said, "No. What is today?" It is the 35th anniversary of the day you hired an English major for an accounting job. I just wanted to call and thank you, now that I am retiring, for giving me the opportunity of getting a job that I truly loved."

This story illustrates an important lesson for the employer by pointing out the important part you play in the lives of your employees. Treat your employees with respect and help them achieve their dreams. Remember, you can't help someone reach the top of the mountain without you getting there also.

Hire a Contractor or an Employee? (Ref. www.sba.gov)

Independent contractors and employees are not the same, and it's important to understand the difference. Knowing this distinction will help you determine what your first hiring move will be and affect how you withhold a variety of taxes and avoid costly legal consequences.

What's the Difference?

An Independent Contractor:
- Operates under a business name
- Has his/her own employees
- Maintains a separate business checking account
- Advertises his/her business' services
- Invoices for work completed
- Has more than one client
- Has own tools and sets own hours
- Keeps business records

An Employee:

- Performs duties dictated or controlled by others
- Is given training for work to be done
- Works for only one employer

Many small businesses rely on independent contractors for their staffing needs. There are many benefits to using contractors over hiring employees:

- Savings in labor costs
- Reduced liability
- Flexibility in hiring and firing

Why Does It Matter?

Misclassification of an individual as an independent contractor may have a number of costly legal consequences.

If your independent contractor is discovered to meet the legal definition of an employee, you may be required to:

- Reimburse them for wages you should've paid them under the Fair Labor Standards Act, including overtime and minimum wage

- Pay back taxes and penalties for federal and state income taxes, Social Security, Medicare and unemployment

- Pay any misclassified injured employees workers' compensation benefits

- Provide employee benefits, including health insurance, retirement, etc.

Tax Requirements

Visit the IRS Independent Contractor or Employee guide to learn about the tax implications of either scenario, download and fill out a form to have the IRS officially determine your workers' status, and find other related resources.

Employment Information

There is no single test for determining if an individual is an independent contractor or an employee under the Fair Labor Standards Act. However, the following guidelines should be taken into account:

1. The extent to which the services rendered are an integral part of the principal's business

2. The permanency of the relationship

3. The amount of the alleged contractor's investment in facilities and equipment

4. The nature and degree of control by the principal

5. The alleged contractor's opportunities for profit and loss

6. The amount of initiative, judgment, or foresight in open market competition with others that is required for the success of the claimed independent contractor

7. The degree of independent business organization and operation

Whether a person is an independent contractor or an employee generally depends on the amount of control exercised by the employer over the work being done. Read Equal Employment Opportunity Laws - Who's Covered? for more information on how to determine whether a person is an independent contractor or an employee, and which are covered under federal laws.

Chapter Nine
Profit Margin

There are two components to the sales price of an item; the profit of the item and the cost. The profit is the difference between what you paid for an item and the price you sold it for. If something sells for $100 and it cost you $60 dollars then the gross profit was $40. In other terms you made 40% profit with a 60% cost; the profit margin is 40%.

- $40/100 = 40\%$ gross profit margin
- $60/100 = 60\%$ cost

Note that both components of the sales price total 100%

What is the difference between **gross profit margin** and **net profit margin?** Gross profit margin is the profit margin before subtracting taxes and operating costs and net profit margin is the profit margin remaining after the taxes and operating costs are subtracted.

Every business has an average **gross profit margin** and **net profit margin** that it must achieve to cover expenses and make a profit. A grocery store can work on a small gross margin of say 25% because they sell in such large volumes. A jewelry store operates on a higher gross margin because of the nature of the business; 60% or more. A retail furniture store must operate at a minimum of a 50% gross margin. A term that is used in the furniture business is "Key Stone" which means the item purchased is normally sold at double the wholesale purchase price. In other words it has a 100% markup which relates to a 50% profit margin.

Don't confuse the 100% markup with 100% profit. There is no such thing as a 100% profit margin unless of course you have someone give you the item. In this case you would have zero cost, so whatever it sold for would be 100% profit. Beware of advertisements saying you can sell their product and make 100% profit. What they really mean is a 100% mark up. I have often thought it would be fun to send them an order, with no payment, saying that you appreciated them providing you with free inventory so you can make 100% profit.

In California I owned a furniture store and attempted to average 50% profit. It was difficult to do because many of your sales were at lower prices which lowered your gross profit average. Also I had a competitor that thought she could operate a successful business at about a 35% profit. She was buying from some of the same suppliers as me, so I knew what she was paying. She would buy a lamp for $25 and sell in for $35 instead of the normal keystone price of $50.00. Her business went bankrupt in two years while mine continued for another 20 years. She didn't realize that she couldn't operate on such a small margin but in the process she caused my business to lose sales because of her lack of knowledge on what it took too succeed in her business. Fortunately she went out of business but there was soon another idiot to take her place. This is something that all businesses must put up with. Many times you can help alleviate this problem by offering superior service to counteract the differences in sales prices.

In the antiques and used furniture business you need to strive for a 300% mark up to survive. In other words, you need to sell an item for three times what you paid for it. (Assume your cost was $100 and you sell it for $300.)

- 200/300 = 66 2/3 % gross profit
- 100/300 = 33 1/3% cost

The 66 2/3% profit may seem excessive but it isn't really. First remember, you can buy new furniture or other retail goods from a catalog or sales rep and make 50% gross profit and have the merchandize delivered to your door. In the antique and used furniture business, you have added costs of traveling some distance to an auction, you may go several days without finding something to sell, you might buy something that you think will sell for a lot of money but on closer inspection, you discover it is a reproduction and won't even sell for what you paid for it. In other words in this particular business you need to strive for the three times markup so you can average the 50% profit needed to survive.

Chapter Ten
Accounting Systems
Two Shoe Boxes-Single Entry- Double Entry

Two Shoe Boxes

Actually, this is not an accounting system at all. The business owner puts all his business expenses, invoices and bill copies, in one shoe box and all his sales invoices in another shoe box. At the end of each week, he takes both boxes to an accountant and asks them to: (1) prepare payroll records and write salary checks, (2) prepare and file monthly and quarterly tax reports and (3) prepare a *Profit and Loss* statement which is sometimes referred to as an *Income Statement*. For obvious reasons this accounting system is not recommended! Your accountant will spend a great deal of his expensive time handling your sloppy business records.

Single Entry

The single entry system is a little better than the two shoe boxes, but not much. You will still need an accountant to handle the bulk of your accounting. In this system you merely prepare your records yourself by summarizing them on what is called *analysis sheets*. You may have seen those light colored green sheets with multiple columns in the office supply store and wondered what they were used for.

Since you will be recording literally thousands of transactions in this system, it is imperative that you learn to operate a ten key adding machine by touch, you know, just like when you learned to type. You will need an adding machine, with a paper tape, large enough and heavy enough that it won't get knocked off your desk. I was surprised when I was hired for my first accounting clerk job that all the clerks were using their adding machines without even looking at the key board. I thought to myself, "I can never learn to do that." I was wrong. In about a week, I was going as fast as they were without looking at the keys. It was amazing how easy it was to learn and if I had not, I am sure I would have been fired.

Single Entry- *Cash Disbursement Analysis Sheet*

One of the first sheets you would prepare is called *Cash Disbursements.* This is used to record all of your monthly checks that were written and what they were written for.

The headings of the columns on the green analysis sheet would be:

- *Date*
- *Check Number*
- *Payee Name*
- *Amount*

Even though the *Amount* is a credit (-) that signifies a reduction in your general ledger cash account, you don't need to put a minus next to each check amount posted.

The other columns are used to summarize the monthly disbursements which are repetitive: {these are debits with a (+)}

- Utilities-Electricity
- Utilities- Gas
- Utilities- Water
- Utilities-Telephone
- Advertising
- Insurance
- Payment of state sales tax
- Payment of Employee taxes and withholding
- Vehicle Expense- Gas and Oil
- Vehicle Expense-Repairs
- Donations
- Office Supplies
- Office Equipment
- Other
- Explanation

As you can see, this will be a quite large report, but it will make it much easier for your accountant to keep track of your transactions and post them correctly to the various general ledger accounts. Even though you didn't post the entries with a (-) or (+), the entire row must balance to zero; credit (-) check amount and debit (+) expense amount).

Single Entry- *Monthly Sales Analysis and Bank Deposit Sheet*

Most businesses will make a daily bank deposit of that days cash receipts from sales or services and payments on accounts.

Even though the *Amounts* listed on this analysis sheet consist of both debits (+) and credits (-), you don't need to put a minus or plus next to each amount posted. However, for illustration purposes, I will show them so as to illustrate the accounting principal that all Journal entries must add to zero.

Let's assume that you keep $200 cash in your cash register. First you count the cash in your drawer trying to get close to leaving the same amount in the drawer every day. Since you don't want to bother with depositing 30 pennies, two nickels and six quarters to keep the original $200 in the drawer, just get as close as you can and don't worry about the small two or three dollar discrepancy. Over a month's time it will normally balance out to only a dollar or two. If it doesn't, someone is stealing from your cash drawer.

The columns that are used to summarize the monthly **Sales Analysis and bank deposits** are:

- Date January 1
- Deposit Amount.................................2238.00 +
- Sales...2000.00 -
- Cost of Sales.....................................1000.00 +
- Inventory...1000.00 -
- Sales Tax Payable................................140.00 -
- Received on Account (Judy Smith)..............50.00 -
- Over and short....................................2.00 +
- Cash paid out of drawer for donuts..............10.00 -
- Cash paid out of drawer for stamps..............40.00 -
- Other ....-0-

Total.........................-0-

Note that the total deposit of $2238.00 is accounted for with only a 2.00 shortage and the entire transaction balances to zero.

Double Entry Accounting System

This is the best accounting system you can have. It can be done all manually, but most businesses today use a commercial computer accounting system like **Quick Books** or they spend thousands of dollars in developing their own accounting system.

When I started a business in 1981, there were no quick books or off the shelf accounting systems available that would handle both store owned sales and inventory owned by others (Consigned). It was extremely complicated calculating commissions for consignors until all layaways were paid off and then writing a computer check that listed all that was sold for that particular consignor. It cost me over $20,000 to have a program written in D-base III. To save money, Microsoft Excel was used to record the **general ledger** entries and create the **Balance Sheet** and **Income Statement**.

The beauty of a double entry accounting system is that all the accounts are forced to balance to zero. That doesn't mean that they were all posted to the correct accounts but you are assured that the accounting equation is always kept in balance:

Assets = Liabilities.

Following is a brief explanation of the double entry accounting system that is used worldwide. It's like a universal language understood by everyone. Even if you contract out your business accounting, you should be familiar with how it works and what parts you can do in house and what part needs to be done by professional accountants. Even if you do most of your accounting in house, you still may want to consider letting an accounting firm handle your payroll records and tax preparation at the end of the year.

I was fortunate to have a very competent office manager that took care of all the payroll records including the filing of monthly and quarterly reports and payments to the state and federal government.

It is not necessary to be an accountant to start a business but the more you understand about accounting, the more likely you are to succeed. You can always hire an accountant when your business starts making money but when you first start your business, you may not be able to afford one.

Try to take at least one semester of accounting at either a college or maybe one of the correspondence courses offered on the internet. I did both. I first took a correspondence course in Accounting from the *International Accountants Society*. The subject matter was broken up into small 20-30 page lessons on each subject. Then at the end you were given a quiz to see how much you had learned. If you passed the quiz, you moved on to the next lesson. If not, you re-read the lesson again and took the quiz again. You continued to do this until you fully understood the material. It was a very rewarding experience to not be in a formal class and be forced to learn at the same speed as others in the class.

The purpose of this book is not to train you to be a CPA, Certified Public Account but rather will teach you the basics by showing you sample accounting entries that you are most likely to encounter.

You may be asking yourself, "Why do I need to understand accounting? First you need to have neat and accurate records to report your income or losses to the IRS at the end of the year. You will be taxed on your profits and even if you make some honest mistakes, you could be fined hefty amounts. So to avoid that, you need to learn at least the basics.

The basic accounting equation that explains the double entry system of debits and credits is as follows:

Assets = Liabilities

One of the most basic aspects about an equation like this is that whatever you do to one side (assets) you must also do to the other side (liabilities). In other words the assets must always equal the liabilities. If you multiply the assets by two you must do the same to the liabilities. If you subtract a hundred dollars from the assets, you must subtract a hundred from the liabilities. Later in the book this will make much more sense when you see that all the posting to the assets and liabilities add to zero because assets are normally positive (debits) and liabilities are normally negative (credits).

Assets are what is **owned** and liabilities are **who owns** the assets. To further explain, we will use something common to your own life. I will use fictitious figures here but you can do the same thing with your own figures to determine what your **net worth** is. Haven't you always wondered what **net worth** was all about?

I calculated the **Net Worth** of $73,500.00 below by subtracting the total liabilities of $116,500 from the total assets of $190,000. The addition of the net worth figure forced the equation to balance; Assets = Liabilities.

You will really impress the bank when applying for a loan if you show how you calculated your own net worth. The general public has no idea how this is done or what it really means.

Cash in your checking account	5,000.00
Cash In your savings account	2,000.00
Home	150,000.00
Automobile	20,000.00
House Hold Items	10,000.00
Clothing	3,000.00
Total Assets	**190,000.00**
Amt. owed on home mortgage	110,000.00
Amount owed on automobile	6,000.00
Amt. owed on Visa Credit card	500.00
Total Liabilities	116,500.00
Net worth (Forced amount to balance * Assets = Liabilities)	73,500.00
Total Liabilities & Net Worth	***190,000.00**

Modified Accounting Equation

The accounting equation now needs to be modified a bit now that we have added the idea of *Net Worth.*

Assets = Liabilities + Net Worth

But again the accounting equation needs to be modified to include the profit or loss that is created by operating the business; which if it is a profit the Net worth of the owner will increase and if it is a loss the net worth of the owner will decrease.

Assets = Liabilities + (Net Worth + Income – Expenses)

In order to explain this we will use some examples starting with the first entry to record the owner's investment in his business. Let's assume the owner is investing the following items that he owns free and clear: *Miscellaneous Journal Entry Number* MJJE A-1 (A stands for January and one is the first entry in January. The letter I is skipped for obvious reasons. It looks like a one.

- Cash................................ $75,000
- Delivery Vehicle.................... 3,000
- Computer 2,000
- File Cabinets..........................200
  Total........................ 80,200

MJJE A-1

Debit (Dr) Cash..75,000
Debit (Dr) Vehicles..3,000
Debit (Dr)Office Equipment,,,,,,,,,,,,,,,,,...........,,,2200
Credit (Cr)....Owner Equity or Net Worth......(80,200)
                                        Total................ -0-

JE Explanation: "To record personal investment in business"

Notice the Journal Entry totals zero keeping the equation in balance.

Now lets assume that the owner just paid the insurance company in January for a full year's worth of insurance. The total cost of the year's insurance was $1200 but we don't want to. record the full $1200 in January because $100 a month should be allocated to insurance expense monthly. There is a clever way to make the Journal entry so that each moth will be charged $100. The <u>CD</u> stands for Cash Disbursements.

CDJE A-1

Debit (Dr) Prepaid Insurance ,,$1200
Credit (Cr) Cash...(1200)
Total...............-0-

JE Explanation: "To record prepaid insurance to Travelers Insurance Company for one year. Each month a Closing Entry will be made to credit prepaid insurance and debit insurance expense. At the end of December the prepaid account will be zero.

<u>CLJE</u> A-30

Debit (Dr) Insurance Expense................................$100
Credit (Cr) Prepaid Insurance................................(100)
Total........-0-

JE Explanation: "To record monthly closing entry to allocate $100 a month for insurance expense.

CLJE M-30 (not illustrated)

At the end of December after the profit and loss amount is determined, an additional closing entry will be made clearing all the temporary income and expense accounts to zero by transferring the net profit or loss to the permanent balance sheet account called ***Retained Earnings.*** The January first of the new year starts out with accounting balances only in the balance sheet accounts. All income and expense accounts start the New Year with zero balances in order to be able to calculate profit and loss for the new year.

Memorize:

Assets are normally debits or positive and liabilities are normally credits or negative. The credits are indicated by a minus sign or brackets around the number itself. It follows then that to increase an asset you need to add a debit to it and to reduce an asset, you need to add a credit to it. To increase a liability you need to add a credit to it and to reduce a liability, you need to add a debit to it.

To illustrate debits and credits the following is a sales entry for the first day pizza sales.

SJE A-4

	Dr	Cr
Cash	2575.00	
Cost of Sales	60.00	
Inventory		60.00
Sales		2500.00
Sales Tax Payable to the state		75.00
Total	2635.00	2635.00

"To record the sale of 50 pizzas and 40 drinks the first day open. Using an estimate for the cost of the ingredients in the pizza and drinks allows the owner to have an estimated daily profit analysis. The errors in this estimation will be corrected when the final inventory is taken of all the ingredients and compare it to the book inventory. The General ledger accounts will than need to adjusted to reflect the actual cost costs.

The sales illustrated here showing a profit of $2440.00 ($2500.00 sales less 60.00 ingredient cost) is the owners' *gross profit*. His *net profit* will be much less when you subtract all of his operating expenses.

Journal Entry Numbering System

- **A January**
- **B February**
- **C March**
- **D April**
- **E May**
- **F June**
- **G July**
- **H August**
- **I Skip**
- **J September**
- **K October**
- **L November**
- **M December**

Cash Disbursement Journal Voucher for January 15th.
CDJV A15

Pay Roll Journal Voucher for March 7
PRJV C7

Sales Journal Voucher for May 15th.
SJV E15

Purchase Journal Voucher for July 22nd.-PJV G22

Miscellaneous Journal voucher for October 20th.-MJV K20

JV = Journal Voucher (group of Journal entries)
JE = Journal Entry (Individual entry)

The following page illustrates an example of one month's journal voucher postings and how they affect the general ledger dollar amounts. The only reason the Balance Sheet beginning balance shows zero amounts is that the business was begun after January 1st. The Income and expense accounts beginning balance also shows zero because it is the start of a new year's accounting.

Keep in mind that at the end of the year all temporary Expense general ledger accounts will be subtracted from the temporary income accounts in order to determine how much profit or loss was incurred for the year. This balance will be transferred to the *Yearly Income Summary* general ledger account. This allows all the income and expense accounts to be dropped so that a new year can be recorded by starting out with zero income and zero expenses for January 1, of the new year.

Some of this may be difficult to grasp until you use a real life situation using real numbers. Once you understand this beautiful system of double entry accounting, you will have much more appreciation for its usefulness in your business adventure.

Again, I want to suggest that you make an effort to learn the Microsoft "Excel" spread sheet program so that you can at least make summary schedules for an outside accountant if you choose not to do all the accounting yourself. The example on the next page was made using "Excel." The program makes all the calculations saving you the hassle of using an adding machine.

51

Acct #	Gen. Led. Acct.	Jan Beg Bal	Misc JV	Sales JV	Purch JV	Pay Roll	Cash Dis.	Close JV	Total
REF JV			MJ A1	SJ A4	PJ A1	PRJ A 31	CDJV A 1	CJE A 30	
1000	Cash		75,000.00	2575.00			-1200.00		76,375.00
1050	Cash register								
1100	Accounts receivable								
1200	Inventory			-60.00					-60.00
1300	Deposits Workmans comp								
1350	Prepaid insurance						1200.00	-100.00	1100.00
1500	Vehicle		3,000.00						3,000.00
1501	Vehicle Accum. Dep.								
1520	Office Equpment		2200.00						2200.00
1600	Store fixtures								
1601	Stores Accum. Dep.								
2100	Sales Tax Payable			-75.00					-75.00
2700	Accounts payable								
2750	Pay roll tax pay								
2800	Owner equity		-						-
			80,200.00						80,200.00

Sample Journal Entry Postings (Pages 47-49)

Acct # REF JV	Gen. Led. Account Name	Jan Beg Bal	Misc JV MJ A1	Sales JV SJ A4	Purch JV PJ A1	Pay Roll PRJ A 31	Cash Dis. CDJV A 1	Close JV CIE A 30	Total
2850	Loans Payable								
2900	Retained earnings								
4100	Sales			-2500.00					-2500
5000	Cost of sales			60.00					60.00
6000	Over and short								
6010	Interest expense							100.00	100.00
6020	License fees								
6050	Building rent								
6080	Sanitation expense								
6150	Advertising								
6300	Utilites electric								
6301	Utilities gas								
6302	Utilities Telephone								
6400	Insurance								
6425	Bank service charge								
6450	Custodial service								
6455	Accounting prepartion								
6650	Salary expense								
	Total		0.00	0.00			0.00	0.00	0.00

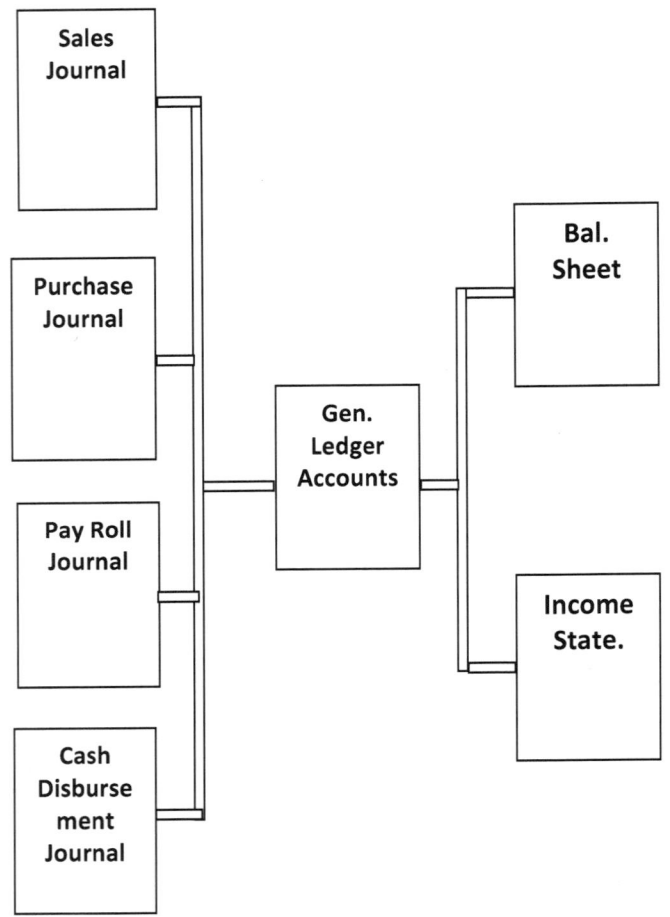

Accounting System Flow Chart

All four of the above Journals may be computer generated or hand generated. They feed, so to speak, the General Ledger. The General Ledger then feeds the monthly financial statements; Balance Sheet and Income Statement. The General Ledger Asset and Liability accounts will be posted to the "Balance Sheet" and all "Income and Expense" accounts will be posted to the "Income Statement." Note: Not shown is a Miscellaneous JV used to record corrections and start up postings like the owners investment in the business.

Balance Sheet Format

Current Assets

	Jan	Feb	Mar
Cash			
Accounts receivable			
Inventory			
Prepaid expenses			
Total Current Assets			

Fixed Assets

Real Estate			
Office Computer			
Office Copier			
Office File cabinets			
Vehicles			
Total Fixed Assets			

Total Assets*			

Current Liabilities

Accounts payable			
Income tax payable			
Total current Liabilities			

Long Term Liabilities

Loans Payable			
Other			
Total Long Term Liabilities			

Owner Equity

Owners Investment			
Retained Earnings			
Total Owner Equity			

Total Lia. & Owner Equity *			

Income Statement Format

Revenue	Jan	Feb	March	T. Qtr
Sales revenue				
Less Returns				
Service revenue				
Interest revenue				
Other revenue				
Total Revenues				

Expenses

Expenses	Jan	Feb	March	T. Qtr
Advertising				
Bad Debt				
Commissions				
Cost Goods sold				
Depreciation				
Employee Ben.				
Insurance				
Interest Exp.				
Maintenance				
Office supplies				
Payroll taxes				
Rent				
Salaries				
Utilities				
other				
Total Expenses				

Net Income				

Monthly
Bank Statement Reconciliation

Just because you don't reconcile your personal monthly bank statement, don't think you can skip your business statement. You must always be in control of your finances and know exactly how much money you have available for those emergency situations. Additionally, if one of your checks bounces that was written to either one of your customers or vendors, your reputation will be damaged which in turn could affect your income negatively.

Your business bank reconciliation is a little different from your home bank reconciliation where you only balance the banks figures to what your check book shows. In your business you want your bank statement to agree with not only the check book but also with your general ledger amount. Don't bother to read how to balance your statement from the banks instructions on the back of the statement. That's just too confusing. Just make three columns on one of those green analysis sheets and write in each amount. The trick is to get all three column totals to total the same amount.

	Bank Statement	Check Book	General Ledger
A	12,678.43	9,234.58	8215.89
B		(12.32)	(12.32)
C	(4443.85)		
D	1,000.00		
T	9234.58	9234.58	9234.58

A= Ending Balance
B= Bank Service Charge
C= Checks not cleared the bank
D= Deposits not cleared the bank

The first think to do in reconciling your monthly bank statement is to write the current **bank statements balance** under the **Bank Statement** column, your **manual check book total** under the **Check Book** column and your **general ledger balance** under the **General Ledger** column as shown in (A).

You can go in any order but for some reasons, I first deduct the banks **service charge** (B) from the **check book column** and **general ledger column.** Don't forget to manually subtract the service charge from your actual check book and prepare a journal entry to subtract the service charge from the general ledger or you won't balance the following month.

Next check off all the **checks** from your manual check book to the bank statement to determine which **checks** have not cleared the bank and then either subtract them from the banks column or add them to the check book column; it will balance either way. In the example above, I subtract them from the bank statement column because it is assumed that most of them will clear the following month as shown in (C)

The **deposits** the bank hasn't recorded, I can either add them to the banks column or subtract them from the check book column; again it will balance either way. Since it is expected they will be recorded by the bank the following month, I choose to record them in the bank Statement column as shown in (D).

The same reasoning will apply to which deposits and checks have been recorded in the general ledger compared to the bank and check book.

It is really not that difficult to complete a bank reconciliation if you have one of those heavy adding machines with a paper tape and learn to use it by touch. Start practicing on your personal account at home. Memorize the numbers position, addition and subtraction keys and total keys on your adding/calculator machine. Always start with positioning your three middle fingers on the 4, 5, 6 keys in the center of the numbers. It's a little confusing at first because the telephone numbers are in reverse. The telephone company apparently did this to keep you from dialing the phone numbers too fast. I can't personally use a really sensitive key touch or one that is so small and light weight that I knock it off my desk when I get to going really fast. Be sure to shop around and try them out first before buying one.

Earlier, I suggested that you understand how to use Microsoft's spreadsheet program called Excel. I used excel to assist me balancing my company's large outstanding checks. I wrote up to $10,000 a month in commission checks each month. For some unknown reason many people would not cash their commission checks for several months and some never did. It was a real pain to rewrite them every month in the Banks column as outstanding checks. By using excel I could copy the outstanding checks from the previous months reconciliation and paste them to the current months reconciliation. In addition to not having to manually rewrite the checks in the new reconciliation sheet, excel would add the long columns of numbers so I didn't need to use the adding machine.

Again, try and learn how to us Microsoft's Excel Spread Sheet and the word processer called "Word." If you don't you are like a carpenter trying to do his job without a hammer and saw.

One of my business customers came into my store one morning looking rather down. I said, "Is everything alright?" "Well, I guess, but I lost a lot of money this month."
"What Happened," I asked.
"I had to buy a huge amount of inventory in January.

I explained to him that buying inventory does not cause your business to lose money. "All you did was to trade a Cash Asset for an Inventory Asset. Both are Balance sheet accounts and don't reflect any expenses. Your cash flow may be hurting you this month but you didn't actually incur an expense when you purchased inventory. We talked for about an hour and when he left, he still didn't understand my point.

If you are going to be in business, you must understand this basic accounting concept.

Chapter Eleven
Advertising and Promotion

Press Release

One of the best promotions is a ***Press Release*** to the local newspapers, and Radio and Television stations advising them that you are opening a new business. And it is free! The only cost is your time and postage. I would send the Press Release by both snail mail and email. You might also consider sending them to several of the larger offices in town to attract large party ***platter*** orders for business meetings if you are in the food business. (See a sample ***Press Release*** in the appendix)

Telephone directory

It is very important that you get your name in the local telephone directory because it is only published once a year. So plan early and not get trapped into a situation where you will have to wait several months to get a listing. You may think that this is not important because most customers will simply look up your telephone number on your web page. You would be surprised of the large number of people who still don't know how to do this. You tell them to "Google" something and they have no idea what you are talking about.

Be extremely careful though to not spend more than necessary for yellow page advertising. The yellow page ad sales people work on a commission that makes them as devious as a used car salesman. Advertise just enough to get by. Don't try to compete with the attorneys who take out full page ads. Remember they get thousands of dollars for settling some of their cases.

News Paper Advertising

Most business will do fairly well with newspaper advertising but it's expensive; especially if it doesn't work. An advertising agency would normally create ads that would be better than yours but again it will cost more to have them do it. If you are not proficient in *Microsoft Word,* I strongly advise that you master it. Then you will be able to create your own ads. Once you learn how to type in word and copy and paste and resize pictures and art work, you can produce some very effective ads. The newspaper will prepare your ad and resize pictures and art work but I prefer to do that myself. What I submit to the paper is *camera ready* and insures that there will be minimum errors. Many times you can copy business ads from other areas and simply change the name and addresses and prices.

The newspapers will give you a better rate if you sign a long term contract to advertise regularly.

Community Shoppers

These are normally distributed free at local super markets, motels, restaurants and tourist stops. They should not be a major source of advertising but rather as a possible more cost effective media. To test their effectiveness use a good discount coupon so you can track the effectiveness of your ad.

Radio and TV

I am a little reluctant to recommend radio and TV advertising, not that they aren't effective but they are expensive. There are so many TV stations now that almost everyone has cable, that the odds of someone watching the TV station where your ad is, is quite remote. If you have a large advertising budget, give it a try but figure out a way to test its efficiency.

Direct Mail

With the advent of the computer this is easier than in the past. For a reasonable fee you can purchase address files or preprinted mailing labels for any particular zip code. This allows you to target your customer base without wasting valuable resources.

You may find it cheaper or at least more effective to use a mailing service company that bundles your ad with others to save on mailing costs.

Website

You must have a web site. If you don't, you will be at a great disadvantage. Your customers will access your website for a variety of reasons and the positive impressions they get will largely determine your success. Simply put, if you have a business today, you must have a website.

"In the U.S. alone, the number of internet users (approximately 77 percent of the population) and e-commerce sales ($165.4 billion in 2010, according to the US Department of Commerce) continue to rise and are expected to increase with each passing year.

At the very least, every business should have a professional looking and well-designed website that enables users to easily find out about their business and how to avail themselves of their products and services. Later, additional ways to generate revenue on the website can be added; i.e., selling ad space, drop-shipping products, or recommending affiliate products.

Remember, if you don't have a website, you'll most likely be losing business to those who do. And make sure that a website makes your business look good, not bad -- you want to increase revenues, not decrease them." (Reference sba.gov website)

Advertising as a percentage of sales

Almost every business is confronted with how much to spend on advertising and promotion. One way is to spend a certain percentage of sales for advertising. The next question; what is that percentage. It is difficult to come up with a direct answer because all businesses are different. For example:

- Automakers 2.5% to 3.5%
- Liquor 5.5% to 7.5%
- Other Industries 4% to 10%

Advertising as a percentage of sales (continued)

- Service business 5% or more
- Young companies upwards to 15%
- Target approximately 2%
- Best Buy 3%
- Macy's 5%
- Wal-Mart 0.4%

Try to find out what the advertising to sales ratio is typical in your type of business. Your CPA or tax preparer should be able to give you this figure based on his other clients or personal experience. If you are unsure, start out at 5% and later adjust this percentage up or down depending on the cost of the media and what you can learn about how much your competitors spend. Be careful though. I had a friend who tried to keep up with his competitors advertising and he went broke. Your competitor may be unknowledgeable and be spending too much.

Sources of Information:

- There are quite a number of government publications available from the Small Business Administration (SBA) that will provide answers and guidance to help you succeed in business.

- Join a trade group that represents your particular type of business. You will gain a great deal of knowledge from them on what works and what doesn't work

- Subscribe to one or two trade magazines in your particular industry. Be sure to attend at least one trade show per year.

Most of your suppliers will have tons of information regarding their equipment and operation.

Chapter Twelve
It's Impossible to Pay off the National Debt
With our current banking system

This topic is not really necessary for you to understand to become an entrepreneur, so just skip it if it doesn't interest you. In fact it may be better if you didn't understand it. If I had understood our banking system in 1981, I most likely would not have started my business Consign It Stores, Inc. in Bakersfield, California. During this volatile period of our economy, I was forced to pay 12% interest on a $375,000 loan and most businesses, including my own, were suffering low sales revenue. My monthly mortgage payment alone was $3,800 a month. Our banking system then was just as bad as it is now except that our national debt was only $1 trillion instead of $16 trillion. Fortunately my ignorance allowed me to purchase a very good piece of real estate and double my money a few years later plus I made a decent living in spite of the harsh conditions.

But none the less, today's business climate looks pretty bleak because of America's huge debt, $16 trillion and growing, and both the republicans and democrats seem to have little interest in cutting spending.

Neither the Democrats nor the Republicans have any intention of paying off the national debt. It is politically more beneficial for the politicians to finance their excessive spending through hidden *debt financing* rather than through *transparent taxes.* Financing our government through transparent taxes, would immediately inform the taxpayer of the folly of the politicians excessive spending because of extremely higher personal income tax it would cause. This would most definitely assure the politicians of being elected for only one term.

Even if our government's leaders wanted to pay off the $16 trillion dollar debt, it is not possible under our current banking system.

Our economy (money supply) is always short the amount of interest that *was not* created through fractional reserve banking. When the bank approves your loan, they create the principal out of thin air but the interest is not created at all. The Federal Government will have to create this money by borrowing it from the privately owned Federal Reserve Bank which charges the taxpayers interest. Again the Federal Reserve Bank does not create the interest; only the principal. The interest, not created by the Federal Reserve's loan, forces our government to borrow even more money. It is a never ending cycle; the federal debt can never be paid off.

The only solution is to:

- Abolish the **unconstitutional Federal Reserve** and allow the U.S. Treasury Department to issue our money supply interest free, as provided for in the Constitution. This won't be inflationary as long as they don't issue more than the difference between the total GDP less the money already in circulation. In other words, there is not enough money in circulation to conduct commerce in a way as to consume the excess production. In order for the people to consume this excess production, they could purchase it by charging it to their credit card, which is done now, or the Federal Government could give all Americans a stimulus check instead of allowing the banks to profit for something they had nothing to do with. This concept is referred to as **Credit as a Public Utility**. Even if you think this is an unrealistic idea, and is unlikely to be adopted, it still helps to explain our flawed and unconstitutional banking system.

- Allow **fractional reserve banking** for only those banks owned by the state (North Dakota is currently the only state with a state owned bank). Instead of private banks profiting from fractional reserve banking, the taxpayers would profit. This profit could then pay for many of the state's public works projects, **interest free.**

- The Federal Government should declare bankruptcy and write off the $4 trillion or so owed the privately owned Federal Reserve. Don't feel sorry for them. They have stolen much more than that from the American people since 1913. (Write off just the amount owed to the Fed and any other banks in the world that are affiliated with them; not individual bond holders.)

- The next step is to finance the operation of our government only through *transparent taxes* instead of through *non-transparent* debt financing. Debt financing should only be used in extreme emergencies, like when another country invades the U.S. or a meteor hits the U.S. and destroys huge areas of the country. Everything else must be paid for thru taxation. Debt financing taxes the people twice; a hidden inflation tax plus the normal income tax.

A side benefit to this proposal, besides paying off the national debt, would be that it would almost eliminate all wars or *Regime change*, as the unelected controllers call it. Just imagine the President appearing on the six o'clock news and saying, "My fellow Americans, the United Nations, not Congress, has advised me that the U.S. must nuke Iceland because they won't allow us to steal their oil or allow the international bankers to take over their banking system. Since we can no longer resort to hidden *debt financing,* we are going to increase your income tax for the next five years, 40%."

What do you think would happen? We definitely would not go to war and the President would probably be impeached; it surely would be the end of his political career.

We continuously vote every four years for both Republican and Democrat leaders that represent the *Banksters* instead of the people. Nothing much will change, until the public understands that our current banking system is unconstitutional and that the Federal Reserve Bank is privately owned, created for the sole purpose of making huge profits for themselves at the expense of the American people.

Refer to the block diagram on page 68 to see how our money supply is injected into the economy by both consumer borrowing and federal government borrowing. In both cases, since the banks don't create the interest, only the principle, the dollar value of the interest reduces the total money supply resulting in the need to borrow even more. It is a never ending cycle that never stops.

This monetary system makes it impossible for us to ever pay off the debt. The more we borrow the more interest is deducted from the money supply making it necessary to borrow even more.

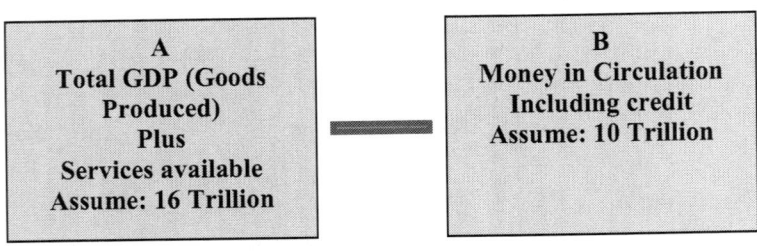

| A
Total GDP (Goods Produced)
Plus
Services available
Assume: 16 Trillion | B
Money in Circulation
Including credit
Assume: 10 Trillion |

C
Gap=6 Trillion
Money and credit in circulation is short 6 trillion dollars making it impossible for the consumer to consume the 16 trillion without borrowing.

Consumer Borrows
Assume one person borrowed the 6 trillion dollar gap so all goods and services could be purchased. Surely they would not have been produced unless it was expected that they would all be purchased.

Bank
The bank approves the 6 trillion dollar loan by creating money (credit) out of thin air. But, it only created the principle and not the interest. Assume the interest is 1 trillion. When that loan is paid off, the 1 trillion will have to come out of the money and credit in circulation, leaving it short again. (Deduct 1 trillion from B above)

> **Government Borrows**
> Since our government prefers non-transparent debt borrowing instead of transparent taxes to pay for expenses, it too must borrow from a bank, often times the privately owned Federal Reserve Bank. Assume the government needs $2 trillion dollars to continue the wars, I mean regime Change, in the Middle East

> **Privately Owned**
> **Federal Reserve Bank**
> Again, the bank creates the principle for the loan but not the interest. Assume the interest is ½ trillion. When the loan is paid off, the ½ trillion will also come out of the money and credit in circulation (B page 68), Again there is not enough money in circulation now to purchase all the consumer goods and services; so the government borrows again. It is a never ending cycle.

Very seldom will you hear anyone in congress suggest that that the Federal Reserve be abolished and allow the U. S. Treasury Department to print our money interest free. Ron Paul and Dennis Kucinich tried but is doubtful they can get the votes to ever get a full audit of the Federal Reserve. Governor Gary Johnson also supported abolishing the Federal Reserve.

Notes:

Chapter Thirteen
What's Your Decision?

I Hope the bleak description of our banking system will help inform you as to the seriousness of our current monetary system. Many businesses will make it in spite of this but it should be clear that this is a very fragile time economically. After reading the previous sections of this book and the description of our monetary system, you should now have the tools that will fairly accurately predict your chances of success. Keep in mind that being an entrepreneur is not for everyone but for those of you that do decide to open up your own business, it can be extremely rewarding.

Early in my life, I discovered that working as an employee would never allow me to attain the level of financial independence that I was seeking. It might have been different if I had become a *"Wrongful Death"* or *"Medical Malpractice"* attorney, a research scientist, etc. Since I didn't have the expertise in those areas and had pretty well bottomed out as an accountant, owning my own business seemed to be a good alternative to seek my fortune.

In the previous part of this book, I described the various businesses that I started and the level of success attained. It is important to note that I was always successful in at least breaking even, like in the TV Facts Publishing business, and made an adequate living in the Furniture stores and Antique shops I owned.

I was my own boss, provided a service to my customers and had prestige in the business community. Individuals, business people, lawyers, executors of estates and the Kern County Coroner's Office relied on me to liquidate and appraise their personal property. This was a profitable venture for me and provided a much needed service to my customers.

As an accounting manager and employee, I was limited on what I could do as far as designing new and improved accounting systems. When I started my own business, the first thing I did, concerning accounting, was to develop what I called *"Comparative Analysis Balance Sheets and Income statements.* The examples of the financial statements Illustrated earlier in this book were abbreviated forms due to space restrictions.

The idea behind *"Comparative Analysis Financial Statements* is that you can see 12 months of figures all on one sheet of paper. This allows you to compare income and expenses month to month and to spot difference and mistakes when the actual figures don't match the Budgeted amounts.

Many business owners fail to recognize the importance of budgeting. They mistakenly believe that Budgeting is only to keep you from spending more that you take in. This is completely wrong. Budgeting allows you to detect errors, like paying a company twice for the same invoice, because the budgeted amount does not match the recorded amount. In the process of explaining all budget variances, you detect errors that could be extremely costly to the company if not discovered in time.

I used a huge tractor fed printer which was large enough to have all 12 months of income and expenses shown, by month and total year to date amounts. Additionally there was room for four more columns; Budget per Month, Budget Variance per Month, Budget per Year and Budget Variance per Year. Since tractor fed printers are no longer in vogue, you can still do pretty much the same thing on a 8 1/2 by 11 sheet of paper if you print in the landscape view and only show one quarter of each of the financial statements on one sheet of paper.

Whatever business endeavor you decide on, I suggest that you include real estate investments even if they don't directly concern your business. If it is not practical for you to own your own business location real estate, owning almost any kind of real estate will help protect your overall investments from runaway inflation.

Inflation occurs when our government finances the government expenses through printing more money instead of increasing taxes. Since there is nothing to back it, gold, silver, or sweat from production, it decreases the value of the dollars in your pocket. In reality it is a hidden tax.

When I was growing up in the 1950's a gallon of gasoline costs $.25 and a silver dollar would buy four gallons. Today with gasoline at over $3.00 a gallon, a silver dollar which is worth $34 will buy one gallon of gas with $31 left over. A paper dollar will not even buy one gallon of gasoline.

This illustration is disgusting. Shouldn't our government protect the value of our money? Shouldn't I be able to put a dollar bill under my mattress today and 20 years later take that same dollar out from under the mattress and buy the same amount of goods and service that I could 20 years earlier?

Our countries unconstitutional and evil monetary system is the root cause of all of our monetary problems. Since 1913, the U.S government has allowed the privately owned Federal Reserve Bank to print our money (Federal Reserve Notes) and charge the tax payers interest for printing their own money. The Constitution provides for the U.S. Treasury Department to print our money *interest free*. Why in the world are we not doing this? Think how much better you and your business would be if you weren't taxed to pay this unconstitutional interest to a private bank.

73

Knowing what I know today, I would not have started my business in 1981 because economic conditions were just about as bad as today. Fortunately I didn't have the knowledge about our banking system and rising debt and I started my business anyway. Luckily for me, my buying and selling of my real estate was timed perfectly to maximize my gains.

The house I purchased in California in 1976 for $50,000 was sold in 2005 for $270,000. Unfortunately the person that bought it from me sold it two years later for $160,000. The building I purchases in 1982 for $375,000 sold for almost double that in 2005. My business, Consign It Stores, Inc, allowed me to invest in this commercial property. If I had still been an employee for someone else, I would have missed this opportunity.

Try to start your business ventures at an early age. If you fail, you will have time to try again later.

One final note: Don't make the mistake in believing that you will be successful because you have a great many friends and relatives that will support your business. In most cases, they won't. There is some psychological reason that they do not wish to be a part of either your success or failure.

Good luck, whether you decide to become an Entrepreneur or the Best Employee ever!

Appendix-

Business Plan (Sample)

Bus. Name **Pizza-Pizza-Pizza**

Name: **John J. Smith**
Address: **123 Easy Street**
City: **Belleview** State: **Oregon** Zip **12345**

Home Phone: **555-123-4567**
Business Phone: **Not available yet**
Cell Phone: **555-123-5678**
Email: pizzapizzapizza@yahoo.com

Location of Business: **506 Main Street, Belleview, Oregon**

Business Organized as: **(X) sole proprietorship ( ) partnership ( ) corporation ( ) Sub Chapter S Corporation ( ) LLC**

Mission Statement

My long range goal is to own and operate a chain of Pizza parlors. Knowing that many business owners have told me that sometimes they make more money owning the real estate where they operate the business, I plan to buy as many of the business locations that I can afford to buy. Of course this would exclude the multimillion dollar shopping centers.

My wife is a registered nurse so we can live on her income until such time the Pizza business becomes profitable.

Product or Services to be sold

We will be selling Pizzas both in our brick and mortar stores and also will make deliveries within 5 miles of our stores. Orders will be taken by both phone and the internet.

Previous Experience and Special Skills of the Principal Owners

I was a manager of a local Dollar store for five years and this last year I worked part time in a Seattle Pizza Restaurant to learn the business. I don't have an accounting degree but did handle most of the dollar store accounting including pay roll and tax preparation. I have computer skills with Quick Books, Micro Soft Word and Excel.

Goals for the Business and Future Plans

My goal is open a new store every three years.

Personal Investment

I have approximately $75,000 cash to invest including a delivery vehicle and most office equipment. I will need to buy a new oven and ventilation hood plus tables chairs and interior décor. The location, we will be renting, is for a sub-lease for three years.

Attached is my break even analysis showing that we have a reasonable chance of success?

Press Release

PIZZA-PIZZA-PIZZA opens January 2nd

To: Belleview Gazette
1605 Main Street
Belleview, Oregon

December 10, 2011

From: John J. Smith
123 Easy Street
Belleview, Oregon   12345

John Smith, a native of Belleview for the last 28 years, has just recently announced that he will be opening a Pizza parlor on the corner of Pine and 22nd street, next to Wal-Mart on January 2nd.

His new Pizza Parlor is in the former Red Wing Shoe store. It will seat up to 120 customers and will be open seven days a week. A salad bar, with a large selection of salad fixings will include barbequed chicken wings.

There is both indoor dining and patio dining.

Delivery of Pizza orders of at least $25.00 and party platters of $75 or more will be made free of charge within a radius of 5 miles. Orders may be called in or emailed to izzapizzapizza@yahoo.com.

John is a past member of the Belleview City Council. His wife, Phyllis, is a registered nurse for the Belleview Memorial Hospital.

America's Banking System

Excerpts from the authors other books:

- *"Billions For The Bankers-Debts For The People"*
- *"Secrets Of Our Hidden Controllers Revealed"*
- *"Against All Odds- President Paul Ronan"*
  (Historical Novel)

These books are all available at amazon.com/books. Search *"Flinchpaugh"* or the book title.

Our evil banking system is causing starvation in a nation of plenty!

QUOTES - FROM PROMINENT PEOPLE

VOLTAIRE (1694-1778)

"Paper money eventually returns to its intrinsic value ---- zero."

PRESIDENT JAMES A. GARFIELD

"Whoever controls the volume of money in any country is absolute master of all industry and commerce."

HORACE GREELY

"While boasting of our noble deeds, we are careful to control the ugly fact that by an iniquitous money system, we have nationalized a system of oppression which, though more refined, is not less cruel than the old system of chattel slavery."

SIR REGINALD MCKENNA
Former President of the Midland Bank of England

"Those who create and issue money and credit direct the policies of government and hold in the hollow of their hands the destiny of the people."

SIR JOSIAH STAMP
President of the Bank of England in the 1920's, the second richest man in Britain

"Banking was conceived in iniquity, and was born in sin. The Bankers own the Earth. Take it away from them, but leave them the power to create deposits, and with the flick of the pen, they will create enough deposits, to buy it back again. However, take it away from them, and all the great fortunes like mine will disappear, and they ought to disappear, for this would be a happier and better world to live in. But if you wish to remain the slaves of Bankers, and pay the cost of your own slavery, let them continue to create deposits."

ROTHSCHILDS BROS. OF LONDON

"Those few who can understand the system (check book money and credit) will either be so interested in its profits, or so dependent on it favors, that there will be little opposition from that class, while on the other hand, the great body of people mentally incapable of comprehending the tremendous advantage that capital derives from the system, will bear it burdens without complaint, and perhaps without even suspecting that the system is inimical to their interests."

ANSELM ROTHSCHILD

"Give me the power to issue a nation's money; then I do not care who makes the law."

PRESIDENT WOODROW WILSON

"A great industrial nation is controlled by its system of credit. Our system of credit is concentrated. The growth of the Nation and all our activities are in the hands of a few men. We have come to be one of the worst ruled, one of the most completely controlled and dominated governments in the world--no longer a government of free opinion, no longer a government of conviction, and vote of the majority, but a government by the opinion and duress, of small groups of dominant men."

Just before President Woodrow Wilson died, he is reported to have stated to friends that he had been "deceived" and that "I have betrayed my Country". Referring to the Federal Reserve Act, passed during his Presidency.

PELATIAH WEBSTER

"Paper money polluted the equity of our laws, turned them into engines of oppression, corrupted the justice of our public administration, destroyed the fortunes of thousands who had confidence in it, enervated the trade, husbandry, and manufactures of our country, and went far to destroy the morality of our people."

WILLIAM PATTERSON

"The bank hath benefit of interest on all moneys which it creates out of nothing."

POPE PIUS XI

"In the first place, then, it is patent that in our days, not wealth alone is accumulated, but immense power and despotic economic domination are concentrated in the hands of the few, who for the most part are not the owners but only the trustees and directors of invested funds, which they administer at their own good pleasure...This domination is most powerfully exercised by those who, because they hold and control money, also govern credit and determine its allotment, for that reason supplying so to speak, the life blood of the entire economic body, and grasping in their hands, as it were, the very soul of production, so that no one can breathe against their will..."

IRVING FISHER

"Thus, our national circulating medium is now at the mercy of loan transactions of banks, which lend, not money, but promises to supply money they do not possess."

MAJOR L. L. B. ANGUS

"The modern banking system manufactures money out of nothing. The process is, perhaps, the most, astounding piece of sleight of hand that was ever invented. Banks can in fact inflate, mint, and un-mint the modern ledger-entry currency".

RALPH M. HAWTREY
Former Secretary of the British Treasury

"Banks lend by creating credit. They create the means of payment, out of nothing."

ROBERT H. HEMPHILL
Credit Manager of Federal Reserve Bank, Atlanta, Georgia

"This is a staggering thought. We are completely dependent, on the Commercial Banks. Someone has to borrow every dollar, we have in circulation, cash or credit. If the Banks create ample synthetic money, we are prosperous; if not, we starve. We are, absolutely, without a permanent money system. When one gets a complete grasp of the picture, the tragic absurdity, of our hopeless position, is almost incredible, but there it is. *It is the most, important subject, intelligent persons can investigate and reflect upon. It is so important that our present civilization may collapse, unless it becomes widely understood, and the defects remedied very soon.*"

CONGRESSMAN LOUIS T. McFADDEN
Former Chairman of the Committee on Banking and Currency.

"Mr. Chairman, we have in this country one of the most corrupt institutions the world has ever known. I refer to the Federal Reserve Board and the Federal Reserve Banks, hereinafter called the Fed. "The Federal Reserve (Banks) are one of the most corrupt institutions, the world has ever seen. There is not a man, within the sound of my voice, who does not know that this Nation is run by the International Bankers". This evil institution has impoverished and ruined the people of the United States. . . . Some people think the Federal Reserve Banks are United States Government institutions. They are private credit monopolies which prey upon the people of the United States for the Benefit of themselves and their foreign customers. ..."

The Fed has cheated the Government of the United States and the people of the United States out of enough money to pay the Nation's debt.... The wealth of these United States and the working capital have been taken away from them and has either been locked in the vaults of certain banks and the great corporations or exported to foreign countries for the benefit of foreign customers of these banks and corporations. So far as the people of the United States are concerned, the cupboard is bare."

"When the Federal Reserve Act was passed, the people of these United States did not perceive that a world banking system was being set up here. A super-state controlled by international bankers and industrialists...acting together to enslave the world...Every effort has been made by the Fed to conceal its powers but the truth is--the Fed has usurped the government."

JAMES MADISON

"The prime function of government is the protection of the different and unequal faculties of men for acquiring property."

"History records that the money changers have used every form of abuse, intrigue, deceit, and violent means possible to maintain their control over governments by controlling money and its issuance."

"The extension of the prohibition to bills of credit must give pleasure to every citizen, in proportion to his love of justice and his knowledge of the true springs of public prosperity. The loss which America has sustained since the peace from the pestilent effects of paper money on the necessary confidence between man and man, on the necessary confidence in the public councils, on the industry and morals of the people and on the character of republican government, constitutes an enormous debt against the States chargeable with this unadvised measure, which must long remain unsatisfied; or rather an accumulation of guilt, which can be expiated no otherwise than by a voluntary sacrifice on the altar of justice of the power which has been the instrument of it. In addition to these persuasive considerations, it may be observed that the same reasons which show the necessity of denying to the States the power of regulating coin, prove with equal force that they ought not to be at liberty to substitute a paper medium in the place of the coin." Number 44 of the Federalist Papers.

"Paper money may be deemed an aggression on the rights of the other states."

ALEXANDER HAMILTON

"To emit an unfunded paper as the sign of value ought not to continue a formal part of the Constitution, nor even hereafter to be employed; being, in its nature, pregnant with abuses, and liable to be made the engine of imposition and fraud; holding out temptations equally pernicious to the integrity of government and to the morals of the people."

ANDREW JACKSON

"If congress has the right under the Constitution to issue paper money, it was given them to use themselves, not to be delegated to individuals or corporations.

"The bold efforts that the present bank has made to control the government and the distress it has wantonly caused, are but premonitions of the fate which awaits the American people should they be deluded into a perpetuation of this institution or the establishment of another like it...If the people only understood the rank injustice of our money and banking system there would be a revolution before morning."

FROM A SECRET AGENT - 1862

"Slavery is likely to be abolished by the war power and all chattel slavery abolished. This I and my European friends are in favor of, for slavery is but the owning of labor and carries with it the care of the laborers, while the European plan, led on by England, is that capital shall control labor by controlling wages. The great debt that the capitalists will see to it is made out of the war, must be used as a means to control the volume of money. To accomplish this the bonds must be used as a banking basis. We are now waiting for the Secretary of the Treasury to make this recommendation to Congress. It will not do to allow the greenback, as it is called, to circulate as money any length of time, as we cannot control that. But we can control the bonds and through them the bank issues."

ABRAHAM LINCOLN

"There should be no war upon property or the owners of property. Property is the fruit of labor; property is desirable; is a positive good in the world. That some should be rich shows that others may become rich, hence, is just encouragement to industry and enterprise."

"I have two great enemies: the Southern Army in front of me, and the financial institutions to my rear. Of the two, the one in my rear is my greatest foe..."

"The Government should create, issue, and circulate all the currency and credits needed to satisfy the spending power of the Government and the buying power of consumers. By the adoption of these principles, the taxpayers will be saved immense sums of interest. Money will cease to be master and become the servant of humanity.

"Yes; we may all congratulate ourselves that this cruel war is nearing its close. It has cost a vast amount of treasure and blood.

The best blood of the flower of American youth has been freely offered upon our country's altar that the Nation might live. It has been, indeed a trying hour for the Republic; but I see in the future a crisis approaching that unnerves me and causes me to tremble for the safety of my country. As a result of the war, corporations have been enthroned and an era of corruption in high places will follow, and the money power of the country will endeavor to prolong its reign by working upon the prejudices of the people until wealth is aggregated in a few hands and the Republic is destroyed. I feel at this moment more anxiety for the safety of my country than ever before, even in the midst of the war."

"I see in the near future a crisis approach which unnerves me and cause me to tremble for the safety of my country. Corporations (of banking) have been enthroned, an era of corruption in high places will follow, and the money power of the country will endeavor to prolong its reign by working upon the prejudices of the people until the wealth is aggregated in a few hands and the Republic destroyed."

SALMON P. CHASE

Lincoln's Secretary to the Treasury who was the pilot of the 1863 banking act in the US never forgave himself, subsequently saying:

"My agency, in promoting the passage of the National Bank Act, was the greatest mistake in my life. It has built up a monopoly which affects every interest in the country. It should be repealed, but before that can be accomplished, the people should be arrayed on one side, and the banks on the other, in a contest such as we have never seen before in this country."

OTTO VON BISMARCK
German Chancellor (1815-1898)

"The death of Lincoln was a disaster for Christendom. There was no man in the United States great enough to wear his boots and the bankers went anew to grab the riches. I fear that foreign bankers with their craftiness and tortuous tricks will entirely control the exuberant riches of America and use it to systematically corrupt modern civilization."

LONDON TIMES -1865

"If this mischievous financial policy [of creating a debt-free currency], which has its origin in the American Republic, shall become permanent, then that government will furnish its own money without cost! It will pay off its debts and be without debt. It will have all the money necessary to carry on its commerce. It will become prosperous without precedent in the history of the world. The brains and the wealth of all countries will go to America. That government must be destroyed or it will destroy every monarchy on the globe!" *Note: The bankers want this to remain a secret.*

JOHN C. CALHOUN

"A power has risen up in the government greater than the people themselves, consisting of many and various powerful interests combined in one mass, and held together by the cohesive power of the vast surplus in the banks."

LEON N. TOLSTOY

"Money is a new form of slavery, and distinguishable from the old simply by the fact that it is impersonal -- that there is no human relation between master and slave."

FREDERIC BASTIAT, THE LAW

"When plunder becomes a way of life for a group of men living together in society, they create for themselves in the course of time a legal system that authorizes it and a moral code that glorifies it."

WN. COBBETT

"I set to work to read the Act of Parliament by which the Bank of England was created in 1694. The inventors knew well what they were about. Their design was to mortgage by degrees the whole of the country, all the lands, all the houses, and all other property, and even all labor, to those who would lend their money to the State—the scheme, the crafty, the cunning, the deep scheme has produced what the world never saw before—starvation in the midst of plenty."

DARRYL R. FRANCIS, former President of the Federal Reserve Bank of St. Louis

"Since the direct method of printing money to finance government expenditures is prohibited in the United states, the monetization of government deficits has occurred indirectly . . . government debt is ultimately being financed by the creation of new money . . . I doubt that monetization of debt has a conscious act . . . I can find no benefits accruing to the whole of society from debt monetization, but the risks are very serious and can be expressed in one word, inflation" "In the case of debt monetization the immediate and even the short run impact is neither an increase in interest rates, and yet real resources are still being transferred from **private to government use."**

Page 24 "Federal Reserve System" Bd. of Gov.'s

"....in the practical workings of the banking system the bulk of deposits originates in the granting of loans....and his ability to make loans and investments arise largely from the receipt of his depositors' money."

"As we realize that banks create their own deposit debts....we begin to see why these institutions are often referred to as monetizers of debt..."

Federal Reserve Bank of Chicago, Modern Money Mechanics,

"The actual process of money creation takes place in commercial banks. As noted earlier, demand liabilities of commercial banks are money." p.3.

"Confidence in these forms of money also seems to be tied in some way to the fact that assets exist on the books of the government and the banks equal to the amount of money outstanding, even though most of the assets themselves are no more than pieces of paper--.", P.3.

"Commercial banks create checkbook money whenever they grant a loan, simply by adding new deposit dollars in accounts on their books in exchange for a borrower's IOU.", p. 19.

"The 12 regional reserve banks aren't government institutions, but corporations nominally 'owned' by member commercial banks." p. 27.

St. Louis Federal Reserve Bank, Review, Nov. 1975, p.22

"The decrease in purchasing power incurred by holders of money due to inflation imparts gains to the issuers of money--."

Federal Reserve Bank of Philadelphia, Gold, p. 10
"Without the confidence factor, many believe a paper money system is liable to collapse eventually."

Federal Reserve Bank, New York

"Because of 'fractional' reserve system, banks, as a whole, can expand our money supply several times, by making loans and investments."

"Commercial banks create checkbook money whenever they grant a loan, simply by adding new deposit dollars in accounts on their books in exchange for a borrower's IOU."

Federal Reserve Bank of Chicago

"The actual process of money creation takes place in commercial banks. As noted earlier, demand liabilities of commercial banks are money."

ROBERT HEMPHILL
Former Credit Manager of the Federal Reserve Bank in Atlanta.

"If all the bank loans were paid, no one could have a bank deposit, and there would not be a dollar of coin or currency in circulation. This is a staggering thought. We are completely dependent on the commercial banks. Someone has to borrow every dollar we have in circulation, cash, or credit. If the banks create ample synthetic money we are prosperous; if not, we starve. We are absolutely without a permanent money system. When one gets a complete grasp of the picture, the tragic absurdity of our hopeless situation is almost incredible-but there it is."

WALTER WRISTON
Former chairman of the Citicorp Bank

"If we had a truth-in-Government act comparable to the truth-in-advertising law, every note issued by the Treasury would be obliged to include a sentence stating: "This note will be redeemed with the proceeds from an identical note which will be sold to the public when this one comes due." When this activity is carried out in the United States, as it is weekly, it is described as a Treasury bill auction. But when basically the same process is conducted abroad in a foreign language, our news media usually speak of a country's "rolling over its debts." The perception remains that some form of disaster is inevitable. It is not. To see why, it is only necessary to understand the basic facts of government borrowing. The first is that there are few recorded instances in history of government - any government - actually getting out of debt. Certainly in an era of $100-billion deficits, no one lending money to our Government by buying a Treasury bill expects that it will be paid at maturity in any way except by our Government's selling a new bill of like amount."

MERRILL JENKINS SR.

"The right of distribution over private property is the essence of freedom." "Force- modern Money, then, has the power to create debt since it can command other goods, but is valueless itself.

Money has purchasing power, but no value -- without purchasing power... Fed. "Notes" must be accepted as a tender for debt, but are not "money" -- so therefore -- do not have money's unique ability called purchasing power, what thing has purchasing power? What thing can force the public to offer its property and rights? Offer means to present for action or consideration; propose; suggest; it is a voluntary act. What thing can 'force' anyone into a voluntary act of offering? The words force and voluntary are exactly opposed and it is by the acceptance of this impossible concept of 'voluntary force' being 'purchasing power' that makes the public believe that something must be 'money' and have this unique power."

CONGRESSMAN JERRY VOORHIS

"The banks -- commercial banks and the Federal Reserve -- create all the money of this nation and its people pay interest on every dollar of that newly created money. Which means that private banks exercise unconstitutionally, immorally, and ridiculously the power to tax the people. For every newly created dollar dilutes to some extent the value of every other dollar already in circulation."

RUSSELL L.MUNK

Former Assistant General Counsel, Department of the Treasury

"Federal Reserve Notes are not dollars."

PRESIDENT JOHN ADAMS

"All the perplexities, confusions and distresses in America arise not from defects in the constitution or confederation, not from want of honor or virtue, as much as from downright ignorance of the nature of coin, credit and circulation."

THE CONSTITUTION OF THE UNITED STATES OF AMERICA

"No State shall enter into any treaty, alliance, or confederation; grant letters of marque and reprisal; coin money; emit letters of credit; make anything but gold and silver coin a tender in payment of debts; pass any bill of attainder, ex post facto law, or law impairing the obligation of contracts, or grant any title of nobility." (Article I, Section 10)

U.S. Supreme Court, Craig v. Missouri, 4 Peters 410.

"Emitting bills of credit, or the creation of money by private corporations, is what is expressly forbidden by Article 1, Section 10 of the U.S. Constitution."

GEORGE BANCROFT

"Madison, agreeing with the journal of the convention, records that the grant of power to emit bills of credit was refused by a majority of more than four to one. The evidence is perfect; no power to emit paper money was granted to the legislature of the United States."

JOHN FISKE

"It was finally decided, by the vote of nine states against New Jersey and Maryland, that the power to issue inconvertible paper should not be granted to the federal government. An express prohibition, such as had been adopted for the separate states, was thought unnecessary. It was supposed that it was enough to withhold the power, since the federal government would not venture to exercise it unless expressly permitted in the Constitution. "Thus," says Madison, in his narrative of the proceedings, "the pretext for a paper currency, and particularly for making the bills a tender, either for public or private debts, was cut off." Nothing could be more clearly expressed than this. As Mr. Justice Field observes, in his able dissenting opinion in the recent

91

case of Juilliard vs. Greenman, "if there be anything in the history of the Constitution which can be established with moral certainty, it is that the framers of that instrument intended to prohibit the issue of legal-tender notes both by the general government and by the states, and thus prevent interference with the contracts of private parties." Such has been the opinion of our ablest constitutional jurists, Marshall, Webster, Story, Curtis, and Nelson. There can be little doubt that, according to all sound principles of interpretation, the Legal Tender Act of 1862 was passed in flagrant violation of the Constitution."

CONGRESSIONAL RECORD, MAY 11, 1972

"Some people think the Federal Reserve Banks are United States government institutions, they are not government institutions, they are private credit monopolies."

CONGRESSIONAL RECORD, JUNE 10, 1932, p. 12595

"The Federal Reserve Board and the Federal Reserve Banks are private Corporations."

JOHN MAYNARD KEYNES
(Chief architect of our current fiat-paper money system)

"By a continuing process of inflation, governments can confiscate, secretly and unobserved, an important part of the wealth of their citizens"

"If governments should refrain from regulation..... the worthlessness of the money becomes apparent and the fraud upon the public can be concealed no longer"

"Lenin is said to have declared that the best way to destroy the Capitalistic System was to debauch the currency. . . Lenin was certainly right. There is no subtler, no surer means of overturning the existing basis of society than to debauch the currency. The process engages all the hidden forces of economic law on the side of destruction, and does it in a manner which not one man in a million can diagnose."

CHARLES LINDBERG

"Ever since the Civil War, Congress has allowed the bankers to control financial legislation. The membership of the Finance Committee in the Senate (now the Banking and Currency Committee) and the Committee on Banking and Currency in the House have been made up chiefly of bankers, their agents, and their attorneys. ...In this way the committees have been able to control legislation in the interests of the few."

"This Act (Federal Reserve Act) establishes the most gigantic trust on earth. When the President signs this bill, the invisible government by the Monetary Power will be legalized... The worst legislative crime of the age is perpetrated by this banking and currency bill. The caucus of the party bosses have again operated and prevented the people from getting the benefits of their own government."

BENJAMIN DISRAELI, former British Prime Minister

"The world is Governed by very different personages from what is imagined by those who are not behind the scenes."

WILLIAM JENNINGS BRYAN

"Money power denounces, as public enemies, all who question its methods or throw light upon its crimes."

JOHN F. KENNEDY

"The great free nations of the world must take control of our monetary problems if these problems are not to take control of us."

ERNEST HEMINGWAY

"The first panacea for a mismanaged nation is inflation of the currency; second is war. Both bring a temporary (and false) prosperity; both bring a permanent ruin. But both are the refuge of political and economic opportunities."

THE RT. HON. REGINALD MCKENNA (one-time British Chancellor of the Exchequer, and Chairman of the Midland Bank)

"I am afraid the ordinary citizen will not like to be told that the banks can, and do, create and destroy money. The amount of finance in existence varies only with the action of the banks in increasing or decreasing deposits and bank purchases. We know how this is affected. Every loan, overdraft or bank purchase creates a deposit, and every repayment of a loan, overdraft or bank sale destroys a deposit."

"And they who control the credit of the nation direct the policy of governments, and hold in the hollow of their hands the destiny of the people."

JOHN B. RARICK

"Mr. Speaker, the current efforts by our Government to hold down price increases have served to focus the attention of thoughtful students on a little discussed facet of our money system, this system, because of a long procedure of miseducation and studied silence, is not now understood as it was prior to the adoption of the Federal Reserve system more than half a century ago. It is based upon debt; has serious implications for the future of our country, and invites what may be the greatest war in history. ... Every debt Dollar demands an interest tribute from our economy for every year that Dollar remains in circulation. These interest costs force up the price of every commodity and service and contribute greatly to inflation. ..."

"Under the Constitution, the Congress has responsibility of issuing the nation's money and regulating its value Art. 1, Sec 8, Cl. 5, in a recent brilliant analysis of our money system by T. David Horton, Chairman of the Executive Council of the Defenders of the American Constitution, able Lawyer and keen student of basic American history, he suggests a proven remedy for our current predicament that will enable the Congress to resume its Constitutional responsibilities to regulate our nation's money by liberating our economy from the swindle of the debt-money manipulators by the issuance of national currency in debt fee form ... We have a certain amount of non-interest bearing money in circulation, all of our fractional currency, pennies, nickels, dimes, quarters, and half dollars. They are manufactured in our mints, and are paid into circulation, circulate freely, and provide the government with a valuable source of revenue. From 1966 through 1970 the amount of seignorage paid into the treasury by the mints amounted to in excess of 4 billion dollars the profit ratio on this type of currency is 6 to 1, or currency 6 times the cost of production. The cost ration for Federal Reserve Notes is 600 to 1; however, during these same four years, 1986 through 1970, 50 billion dollars in Federal Reserve Notes were manufactured by the bureau of printing and engraving and turned over to the banks; not one cent in seignorage was paid over to the treasury. ... Our Debt money system compels the government to spend more than it takes in, because this is the only way we can keep the economy going..."

GEORGE WASHINGTON

"Every lover of his country will therefore be solicitous to find out some speedy remedy for this alarming evil. There is no possible substitute for the loss of commerce. Our first grand object, therefore, is its restoration. I presume not to dictate or direct. It is a subject that will require the deepest deliberations and researches of the wisest and more experienced men in America to fully comprehend. It probably belongs to no one man existing to possess all the qualifications required to trace the course of American commerce through all intricate paths and to those and only those that shall lead the United States to future glory and prosperity I am sanguine in the belief of the possibility that we may one day become a great commercial and flourishing nation. But if in the pursuit of the means we should unfortunately stumble again on unfunded paper money or any similar species of fraud, we shall assuredly give a fatal stab to our national credit in its infancy. Paper money will invariably operate in the body of politics as spirit liquors on the human body. They prey on the vitals and ultimately destroy them."

"Paper money has had the effect in your state that it will ever have, to ruin commerce, oppress the honest, and open the door to every species of fraud and injustice." (Letter to J. Bowen, Rhode Island, Jan. 9, 1787)

"If ever again our nation stumbles upon unfunded paper, it shall surely be like death to our body politic. This country will crash."

JERRY JORDAN, Cleveland Fed Res Bank President

"The failed attempts at influencing real economic activity during the late 1960's and 1970's are a clear warning of the damaging power of the central bank."

DENNIS KARNOFSKY
Chief economic adviser St. Louis Federal Reserve Bank

"....what is a dollar it's just something artificial we throw out there....what you're doing is you're fooling people...."

LAWRENCE PARKS, Executive Director, FAME

"Bypassing voters, taxpayers and the public at large, Congress has delegated to the Fed a power that the Congress itself does not have."

LUDWIG VON MISES

"Government is the only agency which can take a useful commodity like paper, slap some ink on it and make it totally worthless."

DANIEL WEBSTER

"No other rights are safe where property is not safe:"

"Of all the contrivances devised for cheating the laboring classes of mankind, none has been more effective than that which deludes him with paper money."

"We are in danger of being overwhelmed with irredeemable paper, mere paper, representing not gold nor silver; no sir, representing nothing but broken promises, bad faith, bankrupt corporations, cheated creditors and a ruined people."

PELATIAH WEBSTER

"Paper money polluted the equity of our laws, turned them into engines of oppression, corrupted the justice of our public administration, destroyed the fortunes of thousands who had confidence in it, enervated the trade, husbandry, and manufactures of our country, and went far to destroy the morality of our people."

BENJAMIN FRANKLIN

"The refusal of King George to operate an honest colonial money system which freed the ordinary man from the clutches of the manipulators was probably the prime cause of the Revolution."
"The Colonies would gladly have borne the little tax on tea and other matters, had it not been that England took away from the Colonies their money, which created unemployment and dissatisfaction."

THOMAS JEFFERSON

"The system of banking we have both equally and ever reprobated. I contemplate it as a blot left in all our constitutions, which, if not covered, will end in their destruction, ... I sincerely believe, with you, that banking establishments are more dangerous than standing armies; and that the principle of spending money to be paid by posterity, under the name of funding, is but swindling futurity on a large scale."

"The eyes of our citizens are not sufficiently open to the true cause of our distress. They ascribe them to everything but their true cause, the banking system; a system which if it could do good in any form is yet so certain of leading to abuse as to be utterly incompatible with the public safety and prosperity. I sincerely believe that banking establishments are more dangerous than standing armies... and that the principle of spending money to be paid by posterity, under the name of funding, is but swindling futurity on a large scale."

"... we must not let our rulers load us with perpetual debt...If we run into such debts as that we must be taxed in our meat and in our drink, in our necessities and comforts, in our labors and in our amusements, for our callings and our creeds...our people...must come to labor 16 hours in the 24, give the earnings of 15 of these to the government for their debts and daily expenses; and the 16th being insufficient to afford us bread,...We have no time to think, no means of calling the mis-managers to account; but be glad to obtain subsistence by hiring ourselves, to rivet their chains on the necks of our fellow sufferers. Our land holders, too...retaining indeed the title and stewardship of estates called theirs, but held really in trust for the treasury, . . .this is the tendency of all human governments. A departure from principle becomes a precedent for a second; that second for a third; and so on, till the bulk of society is reduced to mere automatons of misery, to have no sensibilities left but for sinning and suffering...And the fore horse of this frightful team is public debt. Taxation follows that, and in its train, wretchedness and oppression."

"I believe that banking institutions are more dangerous to our liberties than standing armies. Already they have raised up a money aristocracy that has set the government at defiance. This issuing power should be taken from the banks and restored to the people to whom it properly belongs. If the American people ever allow private banks to control the issue of currency, first by inflation, then by deflation, the banks and corporations that will grow up around them will deprive the people of all property until their children will wake up homeless on the continent their fathers conquered. I hope we shall crush in its birth the aristocracy of the moneyed corporations which already dare to challenge our Government to a trial of strength and bid defiance to the laws of our country"

"I sincerely believe ... that banking establishments are more dangerous than standing armies, and that the principle of spending money to be paid by posterity under the name of funding is but swindling futurity on a large scale."

"I place economy among the first and important virtues, and public debt as the greatest of dangers. To preserve our independence, we must not let our rulers load us with perpetual debt. We must make our choice between economy and liberty, or profusion and servitude. If we can prevent the government from wasting the labors of the people under the pretense of caring for them, they will be happy."

"The Central Bank is an institution of the most deadly hostility existing against the principles and form of our Constitution."

GEORGE BANCROFT

"Madison, agreeing with the journal of the convention, records that the grant of power to emit bills of credit was refused by a majority of more than four to one. The evidence is perfect; no power to emit paper money was granted to the legislature of the United States."

THOMAS A. EDISON

"People who will not turn a shovel of dirt on the project, nor contribute a pound of material, will collect more money, from the United States, than will the people, who supply all the material and do all the work. This is the terrible thing about interest (usury) ... But here is the point: If the nation can issue a dollar bond, it can also issue a dollar bill. The element that makes the bond good, makes the bill good, also. The difference, between the bond and the bill, is that the bond lets the money-broker collect twice the amount of the bond, and an additional 20%. Whereas the currency, the honest sort, provided by the Constitution, pays nobody, but those, who contribute in some useful way. It is absurd, to say that our country can issue bonds, and cannot issue currency. Both are promises to pay, but one fattens the usurer and the other helps the people. If the currency issued by the people were no good, then the bonds would be no good, either. It is a terrible situation, when the Government, to insure the national wealth, must go in debt and submit to ruinous interest charges, at the hands of men, who control the fictitious value of gold. Interest is the invention of Satan."

MR. PHILLIP A. BENSON
President of the American Bankers' Association, June 8 1939

"There is no more direct way to capture control of a nation than through its credit (money) system."

F.A. HAYEK

"The history of government management of money has, except for a few short happy periods, been one of incessant fraud and deception."

DR. PAUL HEIN

"Freedom and fiat are incompatible; slavery and scrip are bedfellows."

"Inflation (caused by paper money) is an evil which exerts its baleful influence throughout society. Gold and silver were gifts of God, and, short of the labor required to obtain them, were ours free. They didn't have to be returned to the source, much less with interest! Inflation, on the other hand, is borrowed into existence from a privileged clique who, by the very nature of the process, enslave those who use it."

USA Banker's Magazine
August 25 1924

"Capital must protect itself in every possible manner by combination and legislation. Debts must be collected, bonds and mortgages must be foreclosed as rapidly as possible. When, through a process of law, the common people lose their homes they will become more docile and more easily governed through the influence of the strong arm of government, applied by a central power of wealth under control of leading financiers. This truth is well known among our principal men now engaged in forming an imperialism of Capital to govern the world. By dividing the voters through the political party system, we can get them to expend their energies in fighting over questions of no importance. Thus by discreet action we can secure for ourselves what has been so well planned and so successfully accomplished."

Treasury Secretary Woodin,
3/7/1933

"Where would we be if we had I.O.U.'s scrip and certificates floating all around the country?" Instead he decided to "issue currency against the sound assets of the banks. The Federal Reserve Act lets us print all we'll need. And it won't frighten the

101

people. It won't look like stage money. It'll be money that looks like real money." The Bank Holiday of 1933', p20

FRANKLIN D. ROOSEVELT
President of the U.S.

"The real truth of the matter is, as you and I know, that a financial element in the large centers has owned the government ever since the days of Andrew Jackson."

JOHN KENNETH GALBRAITH

"The study of money, above all other fields in economics, is one in which complexity is used to disguise truth or to evade truth, not to reveal it." Money: Whence it came, where it went - 1975, p15
"The process by which banks create money is so simple that the mind is repelled." Money: Whence it came, where it went - 1975, p29

DR. CARROLL QUIGLEY
Georgetown professor
(Bill Clinton's mentor)

"... nothing less than to create a world system of financial control in private hands able to dominate the political system of each country and the economy of the worlds a whole... controlled in a feudalist fashion by the central banks of the world acting in concert, by secret agreements arrived at in frequent private meetings and conferences."

BOB PRECHTER

"I cannot morally blame all Americans for allowing, for instance, the birth of the Federal Reserve System (a private cartel with full control over the issuance of national debt) and the money destruction that has followed. They are simply ignorant about it and don't know what happened or what is happening. They think that prices go up rather than that dollars go down. Unsound money imposes an environment of immorality, which in turn makes people behave in different ways for reasons they know not. Sometimes you can blame immorality for the imposition of bad structures (bad people do it with full knowledge of what they are doing), but sometimes it is simply stupidity. People revere democracy, but democracy ends in plunder by the majority. Are people immoral for supporting democracy? I think rather that they lack a deep understanding of its essence. At a very deep level, I would say that the reason such structures are created is due to both a lack of knowledge and a false morality, which in turn is due to a lack of knowledge."

REP. HOWARD BUFFETT

"The gold standard acted as a silent watchdog to prevent 'unlimited public spending.' Our finances will never be brought in order until Congress is compelled to do so. Making our money redeemable in gold will create this compulsion."

". . . when you recall that one of the first moves by Lenin, Mussolini and Hitler was to outlaw individual ownership of gold, you begin to sense that there may be some connection between money, redeemable in gold, and the rare prize known as human liberty. Also, when you find that Lenin declared and demonstrated that a sure way to overturn the existing social order and bring about communism was by printing press paper money, then again you are impressed with the possibility of a relationship between a gold-backed money and human freedom."

Encyclopedia Britannica, 14th Edition

"Banks create credit. It is a mistake to suppose that bank credit is created to any extent by the payment of money into the banks. A loan made by a bank is a clear addition to the amount of money in the community."

ALAN GREENSPAN

"The abandonment of the gold standard made it possible for the welfare statists to use the banking system as a means to an unlimited expansion of credit.... **In the absence of the gold standard, there is no way to protect savings from confiscation through inflation.*** There is no safe store of value.... Deficit spending is simply a scheme for the "hidden" confiscation of wealth.... [Gold] stands as a protector of property rights."

"This is the shabby secret of the welfare statists' tirades against gold. Deficit spending is simply a scheme for the "hidden" confiscation of wealth. Gold stands in the way of this insidious process. It stands as a protector of property rights. If one grasps this, one has no difficulty in understanding the statists' antagonism toward the gold standard."

*This portion of his statement is not true. A method could be devised by creating a board consisting of congressmen and state's governors that could assure that money would not be produced that exceeded the country's GDP. Larry Flinchpaugh

After reading what these famous people had to say about our banking system, it should be crystal clear that we need to abolish the private Federal Reserve banking system and allow the U.S. treasury Department to print our country's money supply. In other words, interest free U.S, Treasury Notes instead of Interest bearing Federal Reserve notes. Also Factional Reserve banking at the state level should be abolished except for banks owned by the state. (tax payer) This change would allow many states'public works projects to be financed interest free.

Larry Flinchpaugh

Early Business Experiences of the Author

Author's first job was in his parents Pet Shop at 1202 Frederick Avenue in St. Joseph, Mo. c. 1954. This is where he first learned about operating a business.

The most fun job the author had was training the family's chimpanzee, Vicky Lynn. Training is not the correct term, you simply showed her how to do something and she copied it.

The picture on the left is at 3727 Frederick Ave.in St. Joseph, Mo. c.1958. The author worked at the Reptile Gardens and Zoo until 1959

These early experiences in his family's businesses help prepare the author for his future business endeavors.

Small Start- June 1970

The Patio Shop at 4008 Nowata Road was started by Larry and Phyllis Flinchpaugh while Larry was still working for Phillips Petroleum Co. in Bartlesville, Oklahoma. Shown above are Phyllis and Larry making concrete stepping stones next to their small redwood portable office building on skids. They were in business for only $5,000 for the lot and $1,000 for the office building. They manufactured and also purchased additional statuary from other manufactures to sell in their retail shop.

This is a view of the statuary display area next to the office building

Driveway entering into the Patio Shop. This property was unsuitable for most business but was an excellent choice for the author since they had limited funds to start a business.

After one Year the statuary and craft business was successful enough to borrow the money to build a permanent building to house the business. In 1976 the author was offered a job as an accounting manager for TOSCO, the Oil and Shale Corporation in Bakersfield, California. The sale of the appreciated property and business allowed the Flinchpaugh's to move from a $21,000 home in Oklahoma to a $50,000 home in California.

Good Time Promotions

Robby the Robot

While living in Bartlesville, Oklahoma the author started a company called "Goodtime Promotions" and constructed this metal robot to perform at various shopping centers and children's birthday parties. A person would operate the candy dispensing from inside and stick out a large red tongue out of the robots mouth to scare the kids.

On the lower bottom left hand side of Robby was a meter out of an old tube tester that registered "Good" or "Bad" when a person pushed the red button. Most children got a "Good" reading but if thy appeared rowdy or as a smart alec the meter would read bad. That created quite a lot of excitement with both good and bad kids.

The highlight of this business was appearing on KTUL TV in Tulsa, Oklahoma.

Larry, (Professor B. Fuddle on left) and Steve and Mark Flinchpaugh on the far right. This business was only partly successful but the author did learn a lot. The robot cost $500.00 to construct.

Interior view of Consign It Stores Inc. No. 2 store (above)

Interior view of Consign It Stores Inc. warehouse display.

The top picture display area was air-conditioned but the warehouse portion was cooled only by a huge fan. The 10,000 square foot **warehouse** used as a **retail area** provided a very economical cost per square foot as long as you could stand the heat! Having two stores really cuts down expenses because items like your advertising expenses and delivery trucks, etc. serve both stores. Also it is convenient to be able to rotate employees due to sickness and vacation schedules.

Consign It Stores Inc. No. 1 Bakersfield, California
The Wise Buys Drug Store, on the corner, paid a large part of the $3800
a month mortgage payment.

In the 1980's it was profitable to buy antiques and used furniture in Missouri and sell them in California. People in Missouri didn't seem to value their antiques, primitive collectables and used furniture the same as they did in California. The author purchased a used Fruehauf trailer in Kansas City for $1200. (Shown above) The trailer was parked in a lot next to a large auction house in St. Joseph. This provided an excellent storage facility until such time it could be completely filled and shipped to California. When the trailer was full, a local trucking company would pull the trailer to Kansas City and load it on a Santa Fe Railroad flatcar. Three days later it would arrive in Bakersfield, California. This proved to be very profitable plus it provided cheap local storage until it was shipped back to Missouri empty.

Interior view of Consign It Stores No. 1 in Bakersfield, California.

Note the high quality of furniture displayed. The author soon learned that it is just as easy to sell high quality expensive furniture as it was lower quality cheaper furniture. Not necessarily to the same class of people. The higher priced furniture allows the business owner to realize a larger profit.

Author's Antique shop shown above. Note the quality of the antiques. The store charged 40% to sell a person antiques and quality used furniture. Anything less than that will not cover your overhead and allow for a profit.

Authors sons, Mark and Steve standing in front of the Consign It Stores truck in c. 1985 while on a buying trip to Missouri.

Moving back to Missouri in 2005 to retire and play with my antique cars and write. 1931 Chevrolet Cabriolet on the trailer and two Model T Fords already delivered to Missouri. Note the two antique gas pumps screwed to the front of the trailer's floor.

Additional Publications by
J L Flinchpaugh Publishing Company
St. Joseph, Missouri

lflinch@stjoelive.com

www.larryflinchpaugh.com

Www.amazon.com/books

Secrets of Our Hidden Controllers Revealed

November 1, 2009

$15.00

Discover how the unelected controllers of our government control our lives and dictate what we do and think. I dare you to read this book. If it doesn't irritate you, I haven't accomplished my objective to get your attention. Unfortunately, most people are simply too apathetic and too busy to get involved with new thoughts and ideas that would drastically change their **outdated** opinions. Most of the information presented in this book will more than likely be outside your *comfort zone*.

Perhaps you think you already know all you need to know about religion and the important political issues facing us today. The ideas presented in this book may be shocking-but I sincerely hope it will open your eyes and expand your mind. This is more important than agreeing with the author on every issue.

Billions For The Bankers-Debts For The People
June 2009

$5.00

This 1984 informative reprint of Sheldon Emry's booklet will give the reader greater insight into our country's monetary system and explains why we must abolish the privately owned Federal Reserve Banking cartel that has, from 1913, been in charge of printing our money and loaning it to the American government with interest. The U.S. Treasury Department can print our money "Interest Free," making it unnecessary to pay income tax on our citizen's wages.

Sheldon Emry's original book was not copyrighted and neither is this one. The publisher, Larry Flinchpaugh, has added two extra sections to help bring the booklet up to date a bit. Even though some of the information is a little out dated it is still relevant today.

Consider purchasing several at this low price and give to your friends and legislators.

Most of the bankers today have no real idea how our monetary system works. It is imperative that the public understands so that they will not be tricked into another Federal Reserve type hoax.

Growing Up In a Zoo

February 2011

$15.00

Larry Flinchpaugh
and
Topper

This is a story of Larry Flinchpaugh growing up in St. Joseph, Missouri in the 1940's through the 1960's and working in his parents Pet Shop, Zoo, and Reptile Gardens. The facility was located at 3727 Frederick Avenue-old highway 36. (Now the home of The Citizens Bank and Trust Company) The book is full of interesting and sometimes humorous stories regarding his experience in training

and handling their pet chimpanzee, Vicky Lynn. Vicky not only appeared regularly at the Krug Park Bowl, KFEQ TV, daily shows at the Zoo but even had a part in a Harvard Biology training film. Other stories include the part Larry played in the heroic Air Force flight from Homestead Air force base in Florida to Rosecrans Field in St. Joe. That flight saved the life of one of the Zoo's employees, Bill White, after he had been bitten by an Indian cobra. This story was carried by almost every major news outlet throughout the world.

There are many pictures and interesting stories included which should be of special interest to those who came from miles around to tour the facility and to be entertained and educated about a wide variety of animals, birds and reptiles. Even those people who never toured the Zoo but love animals and animal stories will find the stories entertaining and educational.

Vicky was one of the Flinchpaugh family Members. She ate with them in their private kitchen at the zoo facility but had her own sleeping cage. It was very sad when she reached the age of about eight and began to rebel.

Against All Odds
President Paul Ronan

$15.00

This exciting story follows the lives of four members of the Ronan family, from 1859-2012, as they influence the American political system to once again establish a Constitutional Republic

In 1859, the protagonist, Sam Ronan comes to America from Ireland and becomes a telegraph operator in Philadelphia and shortly thereafter, he gets a job in *Breckenridge, Missouri* as a telegrapher for the *Hannibal and St. Joseph Railroad*.

Because the *Confederate bushwhackers* had sabotaged the bridge over the *Platt River*, Sam almost loses his life while traveling to St. Joe on the train. Having graduated from Harvard, magna cum laude, Sam's son Jeff lands a job working for President Woodrow Wilson in Washington, D.C.

Matt, Sam's grandson, meets the love of his life at the *Frog Hop Ball Room* in St. Joseph and becomes a successful farmer and Federal Congressman.

Graduating from *Central High School* in St. Joseph, Mo., Sam's great-grandson, Paul, obtains a medical degree from Baylor University in Texas and then joins the Navy and nearly loses his life when the Israelis attacked his reconnaissance ship, the *USS Liberty in 1967*. Honorably discharged from the Navy, Paul becomes a Texas Congressman and after a ruthless campaign in

2012, he is overwhelmingly *elected President of the United States*.

Each one of the four generations of the Ronan family added greatly to the security and financial wellbeing of this country's citizens. You will learn how Paul Ronan obtained full employment, truly "affordable" health care, a balanced budget, a plan to totally "pay off" the national debt, all in a candid *entertaining and educational story format.*

This historical novel will help you understand the issues and learn what you can do as an individual to help save our country from ruin.

Movie Documentary
"This Is Our Town, St. Joseph, Missouri"
Filmed c. 1954

$20.00

This movie was originally produced by "Robert M. Carson" productions on a 16MM film that was used as a promotional film for the city of St. Joe. It features several prominent businesses in St. Joe in the 1950's and shows nostalgic street scenes in a much different time.

The 16MM film was purchased by Mr. Flinchpaugh several years ago at a local estate sale from a former film collector. After retiring, Mr. Flinchpaugh re-discovered the long forgotten film in a box in his garage but noticed it had a strong odor smelling like bleach emitting from the metal film container. A quick check with "Accent Video" in Overland Park confirmed that the film was rapidly deteriorating and needed to be restored immediately before it was entirely lost.

The film has been shown several times at the local libraries and civic organizations but anyone wishing to purchase a copy of the film may buy one at "Hastings" most of the local museums, the "St. Joseph Visitor Center" and Hy-Vee on the Belt highway.

Specific viewings for local civic groups, churches, and other clubs and organization can still be arranged by calling Larry at 816-676-2565 or email him at lflinch@stjoelive.com.

Letters Home From Civil War Soldier Charles W. Gamble
(1862-1864)
Compiled by Mark Flinchpaugh, April 2011.

$15.00

These historic letters included in this book were written in the 1860's by Union soldier, Charles W. Gamble, to his wife and family during the Civil War. He bravely served with the 12th regiment, New Jersey volunteers, Company D.

A carpenter by trade, Charles joined the Union Army in August, 1862 to, as he stated, "to preserve the country and the Constitution." Several times in his letters he frankly wrote that he might not come back home alive, but he was serving for a just cause. This is a fascinating and personal account of a common soldier's life serving his country and fighting to keep the Union intact. Told from the intimate perspective of a typical volunteer soldier, you will glean interesting tidbits of historical information not usually found in books about the Civil War.

You will come to feel that you know Charles personally as you read his actual letters about his daily activities during the war.

118

From mundane chores to the horrors of battle at Gettysburg, you will experience Civil War life through Charles' own words.

No matter how difficult the hardships became Charles courageously pressed on for the good of the country. History comes alive in these insightful, heartwarming letters written nearly one hundred fifty years ago by Charles W. Gamble.

This book is available on Amazon.com and at all the St. Joseph libraries, book stores, most local museums and various tourist locations.

Index

29015034R00073

Made in the USA
Middletown, DE
03 February 2016